ProductID: PrIIPreKinEduFlash

D1567311

Praxis II Pre-Kindergarten Education (0530) Exam Flashcard Study System

Praxis II Test Practice Questions & Review for the
Praxis II: Subject Assessments

Effective,
Affordable
Help from the
*World's Most
Comprehensive
Test Preparation
Company™*

"Guaranteed to raise your test score!"

ISBN 978-1-61072-715-0

90000

9 781610 727150

Published by
Mometrix Media LLC

The "Leitner Method" of Studying Flashcards for Maximum Learning in Minimum Time

When you start to study a topic you must learn, there are two problems that quickly become apparent:

1. You have limited time to study, and

2. How to prioritize what you study.

Believe or not, the humble flashcard is one of the most advanced learning technologies available. Our brains naturally store information in "chunks" that are ideally suited to the amount of information on a small card.

It gets even better- in the 1970's a German psychologist named Sebastian Leitner developed a "learning machine" using flashcards that can supercharge your success by using the power of prioritization (so you don't waste time) and positive feedback (i.e. making studying game-like).

Here's how his system works. Get at least three boxes- shoeboxes are ideal for this, or even a shoebox with dividers to make three sections. Label each of the sections or boxes in sequence- 1, 2, 3, etc.

You play the "game" like this: all of the cards start off in Box 1. You go through the deck for the first time- if you answer a card correctly, you put it in the next higher box, in this case Box 2. Study any you miss as you go through the cards, but any you miss stay in Box 1. In your next study session, study the cards in Box 2 only- any you miss go back to Box 1, and any you answer correctly go to Box 3. Repeat until you have as many cards as you can in the last box. Then you should have two stacks- one in the last box consisting of cards you have answered correctly at least twice, and one in the first box of cards you have missed at least once.

Then, repeat the whole process until you have moved the entire deck into the last box.

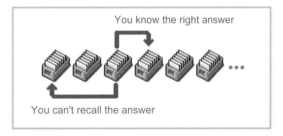

Depending on your time available, you could do as many as 5 or 6 boxes to ensure you repeat the information sufficiently. Research shows that at least 3 repetitions are necessary to guarantee memory retention beyond short-term.

To maximize your advantage, use the system in the weeks approaching the exam to train your long-term memory, then study the entire deck again on the same day of the exam to train your short-term memory. This gives you the best of both your memory functions- why take a test with half your brain tied behind your back?

Good luck from your friends at Mometrix Media!

How to Access Your Free Bonus Material

For your convenience, we have made your free bonus material accessible online at:
http://www.mometrix.com/bonus948/priiprekinedu

Explain Piaget's theory of cognitive development.

Define the following terms: (1) cognitive development, (2) development, (3) developmental domains/areas, (4) fine motor skills, (5) gross motor skills, (6) language skills, (7) personal-adaptive skills, (8) physical-motor development, (9) socio-emotional skills.

Discuss the characteristics of the preoperational stage of Piaget's theory of cognitive development.

Discuss the characteristics of the sensorimotor stage of Piaget's theory of cognitive development.

Discuss the characteristics of the formal operations stage of Piaget's theory of cognitive development.

Discuss the characteristics of the concrete operations stage of Piaget's theory of cognitive development.

(1) **Cognitive development** is the development of the ability to think, which includes understanding cause and effect, ability to solve problems, memory, and reading and math readiness.

(2) **Development** is change that takes place in a particular order that is from simple to complex.

(3) **Developmental domains/areas** are physical, cognitive and emotional areas of human development.

(4) **Fine motor skills** involve the ability to use small groups of muscles to perform certain activities; examples would be fingers and hands.

(5) **Gross motor skills** involve the ability to use large groups of muscles to perform certain activities; examples would be arms and legs.

(6) **Language skills** involve the use of speech to express oneself and to listen, understand, and respond to the speech of others.

(7) **Personal-adaptive skills** involve the ability to complete tasks such as dressing or eating without help.

(8) **Physical-motor development** involves using the body to move (fine and gross motor skills).

(9) **Socio-emotional skills** refer to the control of emotions and getting along and interacting with others; they also include the development of self-concept.

Piaget's theory of cognitive development is based on the idea that, as children grow, they go through certain stages that are in a particular order. All children go through the same stages, but the age at which the stage occurs can vary. The first stage is known as the sensorimotor stage. It ranges from birth to two years. The next stage is known as the preoperational stage. It occurs from two to six years. The third stage is the concrete operations stage, which takes place between the ages of seven and twelve. The last stage is known as the formal operations stage, which can begin as early as twelve and then continues on into adulthood.

The sensorimotor stage takes place between birth and two years. During this stage a child begins to understand certain information that results from his sensory experiences. To begin with, a child does not understand that an object continues to exist even if he cannot see it or touch it. As the child develops, he gains the understanding that objects such as the mother do continue to exist even though they cannot be seen. This provides a feeling of security for the child as he realizes the mother will return. This skill development is known as object permanence. Another skill is the ability to keep a mental picture of an object or person in the mind. Another characteristic of this stage is the understanding that develops as the child realizes that he can cause things to happen, such as pulling a string to make a toy move or shaking something that results in noise.

The preoperational stage takes place between the years of two and seven. It is a period of extensive use of language. A child can use words to stand for things that cannot be seen. Also, the use of symbols begins. This stage's main characteristic is the self-centered personality of the child. They believe that everyone thinks like they do and that the world was created specifically for them. Another characteristic is the ability to understand the difference between reality and fantasy. Children in this stage do not understand that quantity and shape are not related. They can classify objects by one characteristic, such as grouping all of the red blocks.

The concrete operations stage takes place between seven and twelve. It is characterized by a decrease in the self-centered personality. Children also develop the ability to see more than one small part of a stimulus. Therefore, they can group objects such as all sizes of dogs. This ability can carry over to the understanding that pennies, dimes and quarters are all part of the group, "money." Objects that have not been seen or that are imaginary are still difficult for a child in this stage to fully understand. Learning has to be based on concrete objects with which the child is familiar. Thinking in an abstract way is not developmentally possible. A child can put things in order based on size.

The formal operations stage begins at age eleven and continues on into adulthood. It is characterized by the ability to think abstractly and to try to solve "what if" questions. Children in this stage also think about the future. An understanding of cause and effect is also developed. Reversibility, or the understanding of opposites, and conservation, the understanding that just because shape changes quantity does not necessarily change, can both be applied to imaginary as well as real situations. Children in this stage develop a greater understanding of the world and their place in it.

Explain the environmentalist theory of kindergarten readiness.

Explain the maturationist theory of kindergarten readiness.

Discuss the theory of learning of Lev Vygotsky.

Explain the constructivist theory of kindergarten readiness.

Discuss Erik Erikson's first three stages of psychosocial development.

Discuss the theory of transmission of Lev Vygotsky.

The maturationist theory of kindergarten readiness, developed by Arnold Gessell, says that children develop biologically in steps that are predictable and sequential. As applied to education, some believe that young children will learn automatically as they develop biologically. Maturationists believe that children will be ready for school when they can count and recite the alphabet. They believe parents should teach their children these things and then wait until they have been mastered before putting the children into school. If there seems to be a slowness in mastery present, then the children should be put into a transitional school setting or kept at home for another year. The purpose is to give the children more time to develop the needed skills. The maturationists also believe that children will learn automatically when they are ready.

The environmentalist theory of kindergarten readiness is based on the idea that a child's learning is impacted by the environment. Environmentalists believe that behavior as well as learning are reactions to the environment. This means that children learn by reacting to what is going on around them. They are ready for the classroom when they can react in a positive way to the classroom environment. Examples would be following directions and rules. The environmentalists also believe that the best way for a young child to learn is by repetitive activities. An environmentalist classroom would have the children sitting in desks that are in rows. Activities are teacher initiated, and there is little interaction between the teacher and the children. John Watson, B.F. Skinner, and Albert Bandura helped develop the environmentalist theory of child development.

The constructivist theory of kindergarten readiness was developed by Piaget, Montessori, and Vygotsky. It is based on the idea that young children learn when they have direct contact with their environment and the people in it. Also, the children start the activities. The child is considered ready for the classroom when he or she can start interacting with the environment and people in it. A constructivist classroom would have learning centers set up with activities and materials that the children can work with. They move from center to center and interact with the teacher about their experiences. If the child has any difficulty, the teacher provides individualized instruction. The curriculum is also adapted to fit the needs of the child.

Vygotsky developed a theory of learning that was based on the idea that human lower mental functions are inherited and occur naturally. On the other hand, the higher mental functions are a result of social contacts and provide the ability to think in a complex way. Cognitive development is a constructivist activity, and its basis is language. The early use of words helps to form concepts. Part of Vygotsky's theory is called the zone of proximal development. This is the difference between the child's capability to solve problems with no help and his capability to reach a solution with assistance. Factors that impact learning are the internal developmental processes that are present when a child is interacting with his environment, which help to develop skills and knowledge.

Vygotsky's theory of transmission is about education and development. He believed that anyone can learn better with guidance than alone. The zone of proximal development includes everything that is learned with help from another. When one is planning curriculum for early childhood, all three principles of Vygotsky's theory should be taken into consideration. The first principle is that development of cognition is based on age and maturity. Second, social interaction is a requirement for the development of cognition. Third, mediation is also a requirement. The curriculum should include material that is beyond what is supposed to be taught so that the learner's level of understanding is stretched. Scientific concepts are learned through words in a downward format. Spontaneous concepts, on the other hand, are learned in an upward format. The scientific concepts are learned first. Finally, learning involves problem-solving skills.

Erik Erikson developed the theory that there are eight stages of psychosocial development and that it is important to complete each stage in order for a healthy, normal personality to emerge. Also, completion of the stages will provide the skills to relate to others in a healthy manner. The first stage is trust versus mistrust. This stage takes place from birth to one year, and it is here that the ability to trust others is developed. The trust is dependent upon the caretaker's consistent manner.

The second stage is autonomy versus shame and doubt. This stage takes place from ages one to three. The child becomes increasingly more independent, which provides a feeling of confidence and security. If the child is not given these opportunities, it can result in shame and doubt that they cannot succeed.

The third stage is initiative versus guilt. This occurs from ages three to six and is characterized by the assertiveness of the child, which results in security. The child feels that he or she is able to make decisions and lead others. If the opportunities to practice decision-making are not there, the child may develop feelings of guilt and lack of self-assurance.

Explain why development is a result of the combination of growth, maturation, and experience.

Discuss stages four through eight of Erickson's theory of psychosocial development.

Discuss the early childhood enrichment program (ECEP) study and the findings.

Discuss the three principles of growth and development.

Explain why human development has its basis in genetic inheritance.

Explain the concept of the whole child.

Characteristics of stages four through eight of Erickson's theory of psychosocial development are as follows:

The fourth stage is industry versus inferiority and occurs from age six to puberty. It is characterized by feelings of pride and self-accomplishment. A lack of opportunity to practice these skills can cause self-doubt and a feeling of being inferior.

The fifth stage is identity versus role confusion, which takes place during adolescence. This is when the adolescent leaves childhood and becomes an adult. Identity is formed during this stage due to exploration.

The last three stages occur during adulthood. They are intimacy versus isolation, generativity versus stagnation, and ego integrity versus despair.

Development is a combination of changes that take place in growth, maturation, and experience. Changes in growth result from changes in size. The changes that result as a child matures are impacted by the environment and the complex development of the body. A child's development is positively affected if there are many opportunities to learn. If a child uses many groups of muscles, skills are better developed. Maturation cannot be speeded up, but it can be slowed down by certain factors in the environment. An example would be a poor diet. If no opportunity is provided to practice learned skills, development can be delayed.

There are three principles of growth and development. The first one is that organisms get larger in size, and their organization is more complex. Babies grow from top down. As the muscles develop, so do skills. Therefore, a baby learns to pull itself up and balance before it can take steps. The top-down growth pattern is referred to as cephalocaudal. There is also a near-to-far pattern of growth referred to as proximodistal direction. The large muscles and the body's center must develop before the small muscles of the hands and fingers.

The second principle is that growth follows a specific sequence that is orderly. The pattern is based on development that is cumulative. Skills start with the simple and move to the complex and difficult. The third principle is that growth and development are the same for all children; however, they move through the stages at different rates and in different ways.

In 1987 a study was conducted to determine what effect an early childhood enrichment program had on the development of children. One group of children was exposed to ECEP activities, and the other group was not. The study found out that the children who were exposed were definitely influenced by the enrichment activities. They had better motor skills and showed definite gains in cognition and adaptation. Personal-social behavior was also significantly influenced in the ECEP activities group. Finally, these children also demonstrated a high awareness of certain values related to spiritual and moral influences.

The whole child concept lies in the belief that everything connected to the total growth of the child is related and tied together. Biological, psychological and social forces work together in order for development to take place, and each of them affects the others. The developmental areas are physical/motor, cognitive/language, and socio/emotional. If these areas were represented by circles, the circles would overlap. Physical needs, as well as social and cognitive needs, must be met in order for normal development to take place. An example would be that social development promotes language development.

Human development has its basis in genetic inheritance because of the following:

Behavior is controlled by sequences of time.

Complex behavior results from physical maturation.

Growth is the series of events that occur. Maturation is the quality of growth.

Behavioral stages occur as a result of maturation.

Reciprocal interweaving refers to two forces that develop at the same time. They slowly interweave until a merge is complete.

Patterns of maturation are universal, sequential, are found in all children in all cultures and follow a certain pattern.

Explain how the environment reinforces and punishes modeling.

Discuss the general principles of social learning theory.

Discuss the cognitive factors of the social learning theory.

Explain the contemporary social learning perspective of reinforcement and punishment.

Explain the conditions that are necessary for effective modeling to occur according to Bandura. Then discuss the effects of modeling on behavior.

Explain how behavior can be the result of modeling.

Albert Bandura developed what has become known as the social learning theory. It has to do with the idea that children learn from each other by watching and copying. Some of the principles of this theory are as follows:

Learning can take place by observing what others are doing and the results of their behavior.

Changes in behavior do not have to occur for learning to take place.

Cognition is an important factor in learning. An example would be how the expectation of punishment could affect behavior.

The social learning theory can link the behaviorist and cognitive learning theories.

Learning is reinforced when behavior is modeled. The environment also reinforces modeled behavior. This theory can be attributed to Albert Bandura. This can occur several different ways. First, the individual or group that serves as the model can reinforce the behavior of the person who is the observer. An example might be a child who begins to dress like a particular group in order to be accepted by that group. Another way is if a third person becomes the reinforcer. An example would be if a child models the behavior of a good student and is in turn recognized by the teacher in the form of praise. Both of these examples show how the environment becomes a reinforcer. A third way is that the imitated behavior results in reinforcement because it results in consequences. The last way is through vicarious reinforcement. This is illustrated by a group of children watching a video where someone hits a clown doll and is praised. This results in the children modeling the same behavior.

The contemporary social learning theory is based on the idea that both reinforcement and punishment only affect learning in an indirect manner. However, they do directly influence to what degree the learned behavior is practiced. When reinforcement is expected, learning is promoted by cognitive factors coming into play. Attention is also affected by expectation. An example would be if a teacher told a class that today's lesson will not be on a test. The students would probably not pay attention to or take part in that lesson.

The following cognitive factors are part of the social learning theory:

There is a definite difference between what is learned by just watching someone else perform an activity and an active participation in a learning experience.

Attention to the activity is an integral part of successful learning. People learn through the expectation that certain types of behavior will result in pleasant reinforcement and others will result in punishment.

The individual, his behavior, and the environment all influence each other.

There are two types of models—one is a live model such as a parent, and the other is a symbolic model like television, which has images of people rather than live models.

Modeling can result in learned behavior. An interest in reading can be developed by seeing one's parents actively reading. Another example would be the watching of math problems being solved on the chalkboard. Observation of bravery in a frightening situation can also provide modeling, which can lead to learned behavior. Unfortunately, all learned behavior is not good. Seeing aggression can provide a model for aggressive behavior. The development of moral thinking, behavior and judgments about right and wrong can result from modeling also. If a child sees his parent lying to another person, he or she soon develops the attitude that it is okay to not always tell the truth.

According to Bandura, the following conditions are necessary if effective modeling is to occur:

The observer must be attentive.

Memory of what has been seen must be present. Memory can be enhanced by rehearsals of the behavior.

The behavior needs to be demonstrated. If a young child is not physically ready, he or she cannot do this.

There has to be a desire to learn the behavior, which means that there must be some motivating factor.

Because people are different, behavior will be demonstrated in different manners from person to person. New behavior can be learned through imitation. Frequency of behaviors that have already been learned can be increased. The frequency of like behaviors can also be increased. Last, behaviors that have been forbidden could possibly be encouraged by modeling.

Define (1) observational learning, (2) attention, (3) retention, (4) motor reproduction, and (5) motivation.

Explain how educating children is influenced by the social learning theory.

Explain Rogers' belief about the facilitation of learning. Then discuss the principles of the theory of experiential learning.

Explain Rogers' theory of experiential learning.

Discuss language theory development of young children.

Discuss the behavioral theory in psychology.

Using the social learning theory in the classroom can be helpful. The first way is that children learn by watching other people, which would include other students as well as the teacher. Having children talk about what will happen (as a result of a particular behavior) can promote acceptable behavior and discourage unacceptable behavior. This could include a discussion of rewards and consequences. The learning occurs faster and more effectively. The teacher should make sure that attention, retention, motor reproduction and motivation to learn are present. Many different models should be used to teach. Helping students to develop high self-efficacy will promote self-belief and capability. The teacher should maintain realistic expectations—not too high or too low. Teaching students the strategy of self-regulation will help them to exhibit the desired behavior.

According to Albert Bandura in his theory of observational learning:
(1) **Observational learning** refers to the learning that takes place by modeling; individuals watch others and copy their behavior.
(2) **Attention** is keeping one's mind on the modeled behavior.
(3) **Retention** is putting information into long-term memory and then retrieving it.
(4) **Motor reproduction** is being able to reproduce a certain behavior that has been observed; this requires physical and mental capabilities.
(5) **Motivation** is positive reinforcement and the expectation thereof.

Rogers developed the idea of two types of learning. Cognitive learning is the type that is commonly found in the classroom. An example would be learning the multiplication tables. Experiential learning is based on need and interest, such as learning about gasoline engines in order to be able to work on a car. This type of learning is meaningful because the learner initiates the activities, and it is on a personal level. Rogers believed that all people want to learn, and it is the teacher's role to provide the means so that learning can take place. It would include a positive environment, clear purposes, organization, and an even balance in all areas of learning.

Rogers believed that learning would be promoted if:
There is total participation and control by student of the learning process.
Learning is based on practical problems.
Assessment is self-evaluation.
There is an openness to change present.
The principles of the theory of experiential learning are:
Learning takes place if the subject matter is important to the learner.
Anything in the learning environment that is threatening to the self must be kept to a minimum.
Security to self results in faster learning.
Learning should be initiated by the learner; it lasts longer.

The behavioral theory of learning was developed by Pavlov, Thorndike, Watson, and Skinner. It is based on what is seen on the outside (behavior) rather than what is going on in the inside. The theories are mostly the result of animal experimentation that is generalized to humans. In the classroom setting, the teacher is dominant. Pavlov's theory of classical conditioning is based on the idea that learning is a result of association and does not require any personal action. An unconditioned stimulus results in an unconditioned response. An unconditioned stimulus plus a conditioned stimulus results in an unconditioned response. A conditioned stimulus results in a conditioned response. Operant conditioning, developed by Skinner, is based on the idea that the consequences that result from a certain behavior are reinforcing. Antecedents of new behavior plus consequences of old behavior equal learning.

Young children have many ways of communicating with others. Body language, sign language, invented sign language, art, and oral expressions are all used by children. The development of language is influenced by many things. Modeling by others and careful listening to the attempts to communicate are important to language development. By the time young children are two to three, they can use oral language to manipulate the people around them. Boys are slower in language development than girls. Therefore, it is important to provide many opportunities to use language skills for boys. Language development is strongly influenced by the social and cultural environments of a child, the people in the environment, and the actions of the people present in the environment.

Discuss Mahler's separation/individuation theory.

Explain Chomsky's theory of language development.

Discuss the characteristics of the rapprochement and object constancy subphases.

Discuss the characteristics of the differentiation and practicing subphases of Mahler's theory.

Explain the characteristics of Kohlberg's pre-conventional stage of moral development.

Discuss Kohlberg's stages of moral development.

Chomsky believed that children were born with a brain mechanism called a Language Acquisition Device. This is another way of saying that language development is something children are born with. The Language Acquisition Device has to be turned on or activated by using language. Experiences are the most important influences. Part of Chomsky's work showed that language development is much more complex than had been believed by the behaviorists. They believed language development was simply a result of imitation. Chomsky did not understand the importance that thought and understanding have in the development of language and vice versa.

Mahler developed the idea of children progressing through several phases of development, with the first being called the normal autistic phase. This phase is characteristic of the newborn, in which most of the hours of the day are spent in sleep, periods of hungry awakeness, nursing, drowsiness, and sleep again. The reason she referred to this phase as autistic is the inward turning of the newborn. The second phase is referred to as the normal symbiotic phase. This period is characterized by the relationship between mother and baby in which each receives certain benefits from the relationship. Another characteristic is the fear of separation from the mother by the infant. Finally there are four subphases of the separation/individuation process. Differentiation, practicing, rapprochement, and object constancy are all steps a child must take in order to have a healthy separateness from the mother.

The differentiation subphase begins at about five months. The infant begins to stay awake more and is more aware of its surroundings. The subphase continues until about eight months. This is a period when the child begins to reach for things and touch them. At this point a child begins to realize that the mother is a separate object.

The practicing subphase takes place from nine or ten months of age to 16 or 18 months. It could be called the toddler subphase. Major characteristics of this period are the developments of many motor skills such as crawling and walking. It is a period when the child has more interest in touching and investigating things other than the mother. Feelings of excitement and joy develop as well as cognitive, vocal, and perceptual skills. The child is practicing the skills necessary for individuation.

During the rapprochement phase, the child forgets his interest in other things, and once again the mother is considered to be the most important part of his life. This is characterized by "clingy" behavior and not wanting to play by himself. The children who are going through this subphase have many strong feelings of sadness. Rapprochement starts around 18 months and can last until 30 months. It is also a time for extreme emotional upheaval because the child is battling the desire to be one with the mother but realizing that this is not possible, along with his wanting to cling to her but also wishing to be independent.

The object constancy subphase occurs when the child develops the ability to carry the image of his mother in his mind. Then, he can go into another room, and the child is okay with this.

Lawrence Kohlberg developed the theory relating to stages of moral development. There are six stages in the theory, which are put into three groups of levels. These groups are known as pre-conventional, conventional, and post-conventional. The basis of the theory is that moral reasoning is developmentally sequential. Backward steps are rare as well as skipping stages. Kohlberg believed that moral development was influenced by beliefs about justice. The pre-conventional stage is characterized by the feelings of "what's in it for me?" The conventional stage is characterized by the attitude of "good boys and girls" followed by attitudes of "law and order." The post-conventional stage is characterized by feelings related to conscience.

The pre-conventional stage or level of moral development is usually seen in children, but adults can also demonstrate this level. They have a self-centered mindset. To begin with, a child will look at his actions only in the light of what kind of effects will the actions have for himself. Also, children do not see that others have a right to their viewpoints. As a matter of fact, there are not other viewpoints. Toward the end of this stage, a limited recognition of the needs of others begins to occur. This is only seen in connection to how the recognition will help them. There are no feelings of loyalty or true respect.

Explain the characteristics of Kohlberg's post-conventional stage of moral development.

Explain the characteristics of Kohlberg's conventional stage of moral development.

Explain Werner's view of data processing.

Discuss the organismic and comparative theory of Heinz Werner.

Discuss the overview of pre-kindergarten guidelines regarding language and early literacy.

Discuss the S-O-R theory.

The conventional stage or level of moral development occurs during adolescence and adulthood. Morality is based on what society sees as right and expected. The first part of this stage is characterized by the person wanting to be accepted by society. The consequences of one's moral acceptance would be in the form of respect. What one intends to do is also an important influence on reasoning and moral actions. The last part of this stage is characterized by an understanding that laws are designed to protect the whole society, not just one individual. Also, this stage includes the belief that if one breaks a law, it is wrong and should be punished. It is now the responsibility of the individual to follow and promote laws and rules of morality.

The post-conventional stage of moral development consists of two levels. The first of the two levels is characterized by the belief that not everyone has the same opinions and values, and that they have that right and should be respected for such. Also, the viewpoint regarding laws changes from seeing them as edicts from the government to contracts that should promote the most good for the most people. This stage is the foundation for a democratic government. The last level of the post-conventional stage has its basis in universal principles of ethics. Laws are supposed to be fair and just. If they are not, then they should not be obeyed. Also, action is a result of mental considerations as to what should be done if you were the other fellow. This promotes the idea that actions are a result of understanding what is right and not just expected.

The organismic and comparative theory of Heinz Werner is based on the following principles:
A. Orthogenic Principle:
    1. Differentiation: cells become tissues, which become organs, which become systems.
    2. Hierarchic integration: organs group together to form systems.
    3. Growth: tissues, organs, and the individual change in size.
    4. End state: final process of development
B. **Self-object Differentiation**: separation of self from the environment in the following steps
    1. Sensori-motor and affective level: little notice of surroundings
    2. Perceptual level: surroundings are noticed but only as how they relate to self
    3. Conceptual level: abstract reasoning and reacting to the environment
C. **Microgenesis**: problem-solving process
D. **Microgenetic Mobility**: reversal of microgenesis
E. **Comparative Approach**: comparison of differences in behavior
F. **Organismic Orientation**: looking at things as a whole
G. **Interactionism**: looking at the effects of multiple factors
H. **Equilibrium and Disequilibrium**: alternate stages of development of balance with surroundings
I. **Critical Periods**: weaning, resistance, and pubescence

First, Werner believed in the syncretic versus discrete processing of data. Syncretic is a connecting process. Examples of such linking can be seen in children's perception of time. They do not see time as what is on the clock, but as events that take place, such as lunchtime. Another example of this linking has to do with children's perception of space, which is tied up with emotions not in measurements or directions. Children develop the capability to construct an image in their mind. This is called eidetic imagery. They also refer to objects in a certain context, such as "Mommy's car." Physiognomic perception is the giving of human characteristics to inanimate objects. Synesthesia is the act of some occurrence creating an emotion, such as sad music.
Werner saw language as a group of symbol formations that begin as an activity of body action. Pointing would be an example, as well as imitations of motors. Physiognomic symbols refer to changes in the volume and speed of the voice.

The **S-O-R** theory relates to the theory of behaviorism. S stands for stimulus. O stands for organism, and R stands for response. The abilities and motivational factors of each individual need to be considered. Basic behaviorism only considers conditioning and reflexes that last for a brief period of time. Behaviorism also includes how learning takes place in addition to what causes learning. This could explain some methods for handling classrooms of students who are not well disciplined. Behaviorism's most important concept for educators is the use of instructional technology.

Young children's experiences with language and literacy form the foundation for their success or failure later in school. Many experiences with language activities and printed materials need to be provided for three- and four-year-olds. Vocabulary, more complex language skills, and general knowledge regarding their environment develop. Listening skills are also developed. An appreciation of books along with a phonetic awareness emerges. Cognitive and motor skills and social and emotional areas should be included in this learning. Children's native language along with any physical impairments should be taken into consideration. The native language should be the stepping stone to the development of English as second language.

Discuss the development of vocabulary in Pre-K children.

Discuss the correlation of listening comprehension, speech production and discrimination to language and early literacy development.

Discuss the development of phonological awareness.

Discuss the development of verbal expression in Pre-K children.

Explain the characteristics of the development regarding knowledge about literary forms.

Discuss the development of print and book awareness.

Pre-K children are developing a better understanding of what they hear conversationally as well as stories that have been read to them. Some of them are even able to respond to simple questions with one-word answers. Their attention span is growing longer, and they are able to listen for different purposes, such as finding out what happens at the end of the story. Following simple directions is another listening skill that is age-appropriate. These children enjoy listening to stories, tapes, and records. They indicate understanding by their actions. The ability to take part in a conversation is also developing.

This is a time when children's vocabulary enlarges at a high rate. Understanding and using words is an indicator of experiences and knowledge of their environment. Experiences provide the groundwork for the development of concepts. This results in the enlargement of the vocabulary and the further understanding of previously learned words. These words are used in communication on a daily basis. If the child's vocabulary will not provide the means to communicate a particular idea, he will borrow words so that communication can take place. As he experiences new ideas and activities, a greater vocabulary development is seen regarding previous topics that have been experienced.

Pre-K children are refining their abilities to use language to communicate. Language is also used in play activities. This is a period in which the children make up or invent words and use incorrect grammar generalizations. Other characteristics include:
Sentence length is increased to three or more words.
The child is able to tell a story.
The ability to relate to a topic that is being discussed develops.
Conversation skills begin to develop.
The ability to tell a story in the proper sequence is demonstrated.

Phonological awareness means that one is aware that the sounds of words have meanings. This is the beginning of the understanding that groups of letters have specific sounds, and that groups of letters form words. Pre-K children are beginning to develop a knowledge of rhyming words and sounds. They enjoy songs and games that use these skills. Also, they can identify words that begin with the same sound. Hearing syllables in words is developing, and the child can clap along with the syllables in a word. Pre-K children also are developing the skill of inventing new words by changing or substituting sounds.

The Pre-K child begins to understand that print has some meaning. The characteristics of this awareness are as follows:
Understanding that reading and writing provide a means to get information
Develops the understanding that messages are in the form of print such as signs and labels
Understanding that there is a difference between letters and numbers
Begins to understand that pictures cannot be read
Sees that books have titles and authors
Beginning understanding of print orientation—left to right and top to bottom
Beginning understanding that letters form words, and words are separated by spaces
Can follow the print as it is read by another person
Begins to understand that printed words have different purposes, such as recipes or letters

Some of the characteristics of developing knowledge about literary form are:
The child can identify familiar books by what is on their covers.
The child makes selections of books based on his personal interests.
An understanding regarding the differences in books and other printed materials develops.
The child begins the ability to identify story characters, predict what is going to happen, and understand the plot and eventual resolution of the problem.
The child begins to use story language such as "Once upon a   time . . ."
The child questions information in books.
The child correlates books with his own environment.
The child begins the ability to retell the story.
The child appreciates patterns of repetition.

Discuss the development of understanding of numbers and operations by the Pre-K child.

Discuss the development of written expression in the Pre-K child.

Discuss the development of the concept of measurement in the Pre-K child.

Discuss the understanding of patterns, geometry, and spatial sense in the Pre-K child.

Discuss the development of science processes in the Pre-K child.

Discuss the development of the skills of classification and data collection for the Pre-K child.

Pre-K children are developing an interest in writing and will often try to write, pretend to write, or ask someone to write letters for them. The abilities regarding written expression are as follows:
Try to write messages during play
Attempt to write their name
Try to connect letters and sounds
Begin to understand that written words communicate meaning
Begin to try using different written forms such as "wish" lists or stories
Begin to dictate a story or letter for an adult to write

The skill of understanding numbers and their operations is the key to successful experiences in mathematics. Some of the developmental skills of the Pre-K child are as follows:
Can arrange sets of objects one to one
Can count to ten
Can count objects from one to five
Begins to grasp the concepts of "equal to," "more than," and "less than"
Begins to be able to name the number of two to three objects with counting them
Understands the idea of zero as being none
Begins to understand the concepts of parts and wholes
Begins to understand the concept of first and last
Is able to group objects and then tell how many

The Pre-K child is able to:
Clap, stomp, clap, stomp as he imitates a pattern sound
See a pattern of colors; is able to reproduce this pattern
Begin to identify patterns in the environment such as night following day
Begin to be able to see what will come next in a pattern
Identify shapes like circles and squares
Develop an understanding of concepts such as inside, above, next to
See when the direction of an object is changed
Start to explore the results of putting shapes together
Put more complex puzzles together

The Pre-K child's skills regarding measurement include:
Being able to take shapes and place them over a designated area
Beginning to compare shapes (taller than, etc.)
Starting to pretend like he is measuring
Filling shapes with things like water
Beginning to think in terms of time such as tonight or in the morning
Beginning to sort things by size or order things from largest to smallest or vice versa

Young children begin to see the similarities in objects at this age. They begin to classify according to color, size, shape, etc. As they develop this skill they then share the information with others. Some of the characteristics of the classification and data collection skills are as follows:
The Pre-K child can match similar objects.
The Pre-K child can classify objects according to likeness and difference.
These children can sort objects according to set criteria and provide an explanation.
They can create picture graphs as well as actual bar and circle graphs.

Some of the characteristics of developmental processes in science are as follows:
The Pre-K child develops knowledge about safety and use of materials.
The child begins to ask questions about things in his world.
The child begins to be interested in the unknown.
He is able to use several senses to investigate.
He can describe what he has observed.
The child can use simple scientific investigation tools.
The child can manipulate equipment and use scientific measuring tools.
He can describe likenesses and differences.
The Pre-K child can group objects and explain the reasoning.
He tries to explain things that happen.
The Pre-K child can design a simple project as well as create charts to display data.
By using pictures or play, the child can share what he has learned or discovered.

Describe the personal and social development of Pre-K children.

Describe the development of health and safety concepts for Pre-K children.

Describe the mental development of children by age.

Describe the development of technology skills of the Pre-K child.

Describe the social development of children by age.

Describe the emotional development of children by age.

Pre-K children:

Understand the importance of brushing teeth, etc.
Begin to follow certain health routines such as washing hands
Start to develop an understanding regarding the importance of rest and exercise
Develop a better use of eating utensils
Begin to choose healthy foods
Are able to make a healthy snack
Understand the dangers of things like fire
Understand the seriousness of a fire drill
Understand how to get help in an emergency
Understand safety when crossing a street
Know and understand the poison symbol
Understand not to eat things that are not food, dangers of poisonous substances, dangers of interacting with strangers, dangers of taking medicine without adult supervision, and safe actions around water

The characteristics that are related to personal development of Pre-K children are as follows:
Development of a need for personal space
Ability to communicate interests and self-direction
Development of self-control
Showing a personal responsibility for behavior
Development of better ability for self-control
The characteristics that are related to social development of Pre-K children are as follows:
Sharing and cooperation
Respect for others
Friendship development
Using language to express and communicate
Listening to the opinions of others

The Pre-K child:

Understands the use of computer programs and is able to open and close programs
Uses mouse, keyboard, voice recorder or touching screen to input information
Develops an understanding of computer technology such as mouse, printer, keyboard, CD-ROM
Is able to follow pictorial clues to perform certain activities
Listens and interacts with electronic information
Is able to use various software to extend learning experiences
The Pre-K child should be exposed to computers as much as possible because through their use, their learning can be greatly enriched.
The programs used should be fun and age-appropriate but also challenging.

The mental development of children aged 2–3 years includes:
Longer attention span
Words not as easy to understand as actions
Typified by short memory
Cannot differentiate between real and imaginary
Total belief in everything that is said
Choices can be made between two things
The mental development of children aged 4–5 years includes:
Attention span extending to as long as 10 minutes
Observation as the basis of reasoning
Little understanding of cause and effect
Great imagination
Little understanding of motivation for actions

The emotional development of children aged 2–3 years includes:
High curiosity
Repetitive routines
Teasing not understood
Result of correction is temper tantrum
Biting, crying and kicking signaling frustration
The emotional development of children aged 4–5 years includes:
Development of moral attitudes
Trying to distinguish between real and imaginary
Development of awareness of how he is perceived by others
Motivated by praise

The social development of children aged 2–3 years includes:
Self-centeredness
Ability to wait for his turn and awareness of others' rights with a little help
Formation of attitude toward authority
Strong desire to help and please others
Easily over-stimulated
The social development of children aged 3–4 years includes:
Adult imitation
Bossiness
Ability to share with one to two others
Beginning to develop a sense of fairness

Explain how strong emotions influence emotional development of young children.

Explain the importance of caring relationships in healthy social development of children.

List warning signs that may flag concern regarding social/emotional development of Pre-K children.

Explain the importance of social/emotional well-being to the readiness for school.

Describe the risks of poor social development of children.

List some strategies that promote social and emotional well-being of young children.

Caring relationships in which there is intimacy is the foundation for a healthy social development. Social development refers to the formation of relationships with others in which value is placed. The stages of social development are based on completing a stage that then becomes the foundation for the next stage; therefore, they must be completed sequentially. Children's feelings about different situations are based on adult responses and support. It is with adult support that a child learns how to express his own opinions as well as how to deal with conflict. Children feel more free to explore and experience new situations when a safe and secure relationship exists with an adult. It is here that they learn how to share and cooperate.

The emotions of Pre-K children are highly connected to what they think is going to happen in the future, what they think others are doing, and how they see their own experiences. They can begin to manage their emotions at this time. It is also a period of anticipating emotions and being able to talk about the emotions. Also, they begin to develop feelings of empathy for others. The strong emotions such as delight, fury, and distress can highly influence the experiences that Pre-K children have. The development of emotions is closely correlated to social development because the emotions have to do with how the child sees himself and others.

Children who have the following skills are more likely to be successful students:
Ability to point out specific emotions in themselves as well as others.
Positive relationships between the child and the teacher as well as the peers
Ability to control emotions and actions in upsetting situations
Enthusiasm about learning
Ability to concentrate and pay attention as well as work independently in a classroom

The following warning signs may require more information, consultation or referral:
Little preference for parents or caregivers, or an excess of dependence on the same
No fear of strangers
Overly irritable or fearful
Expression that is limited or inappropriate
Little interest or curiosity in the environment
Sad or withdrawn
Sexual behavior that is not appropriate
Excessive fears
Frequent nightmares
Excessive tantrums
Developmentally slow in language development
Obsessive desire for cleanliness and order

Teachers and caregivers of young children can promote their social and emotional well-being by practicing the following:
Develop good relationships with the parents. Always treat them with respect and empathize with their feelings. Listen to their concerns. Build feelings of trust.
Assist the parents in being aware of the development of the child and help them to use developmentally correct materials.
Provide ideas for the parents as to what kinds of things they can do to help the child at home. Ideas and strategies that foster developmental skills by using encouragement are helpful.
Observe interactions between the child and parent or caregiver. When meetings are scheduled, it may be helpful to have both the child and the parents together. Also, be observant regarding the child's hygiene and how his other needs are being met.
If there is any indication that a child's needs are not being met, seek expert help immediately.

Young children who do not develop socially or who lack social skills are at risk for many failures. Being a school drop-out is one risk. Mental health that is abnormal and employment failures are risks. School difficulties that include low achievement can also result. The ability to get along with other children is considered to be more of an indicator of success in school than I.Q. Some experts feel that unless a child has developed a certain level of social skills by age six, he will be at risk all his life. Children who are not able to make and keep friends later find that they are unable to make a place for themselves in the workplace. Early childhood classrooms should monitor social development skills by using periodic checklists and informal assessments.

Discuss some of the individual and peer relationship attributes that will be seen on a social development checklist.

Explain the guidelines for using a social attributes checklist.

Define (1) adaptation, (2) assimilation, (3) accommodation, (4) classification, (5) class inclusion, (6) conservation, (7) decentration, (8) egocentrism, (9) operation, (10) schema, (11) stage.

Discuss some of the social skill attributes that may be seen on a social development checklist.

Explain self-regulation, self-instruction, self-monitoring, and self-reinforcement.

Explain the meaning of self-efficacy and how it affects behavior.

Preschool teachers should assess social development every 3–4 months. Then they should meet with the parents to explain what the assessments mean. Also, the assessment should not cover just one small window in time but a period of observation lasting 3–4 weeks because children can have bad days. The most important thing to keep in mind is quality rather than quantity. Teachers should remember shyness can make a difference in the number of social contacts a child has. A good social attributes checklist will promote the term "usually," which is a key to judging social development. If a child usually performs well, then it can be assumed that he will outgrow any difficulties that may be present. On the other hand, if a child does not do well on a number of the indicators, there is reason for concern and intervention.

Some of the individual attributes that may be seen on a social development checklist are as follows:
Usually in a good state of mind
Not overly dependent on adults
Usually wants to come to the classroom
Usually deals with upsets in a healthy way
Able to empathize
Good friendships with at least two other children
Perceives humor
Not overly lonely
Some of the peer relationship attributes are as follows:
Usually accepted by peers
Occasional interactions, at least, with other children

Some of the social skills attributes are as follows:
Positive interactions with others
Clear expressions of likes and dislikes
Appropriate assertiveness
Not intimidated
Appropriate expressions of anger and frustration
Plays and works well with others
Enters play and conversations
Takes turns
Interested in other children and adults
Negotiates and compromises
Not a show-off
Accepts and is accepted by others
Exhibits non-verbal communication with others such as waving, etc.

(1) **Adaptation** is adjusting to one's environment through assimilation and accommodation.
(2) **Assimilation** is to adopt ideas and information even if it means changing.
(3) **Accommodation** is the result of the change brought about by assimilation.
(4) **Classification** is grouping objects based upon specific criteria such as size.
(5) **Class inclusion** is the idea that an object can be a part of set and a sub-set, such as a dog can be part of the set, "animals" and the subset, "mammals."
(6) **Conservation** is the understanding that objects remain the same even if their arrangement or appearance is changed.
(7) **Decentration** is being able to change from one method of classification to another.
(8) **Egocentrism** is a way of thinking in which you and what you want are the most important factors in the world.
(9) **Operation** is working out a problem in your head; children in the sensorimotor and preoperational stages cannot do this.
(10) **Schema** is having a set of ideas in one's mind that fit together.
(11) **Stage** is a period in the development of a child.

Another way of explaining self-efficacy would be to refer to it as self-confidence about learning. Children are more apt to try certain activities if they feel they will be successful. Most of the time, only activities that do bring joy or success will be attempted. Also, effort and persistence are normally only present in activities that are considered to be successful. A child with high self-efficacy will usually also be more successful in school. Children normally have a pretty accurate picture of their own abilities. Therefore, if a child sees himself as not very successful, he will have low self-efficacy. Some things that could promote self-efficacy in children are their past successes and failures, as well as the same things seen in others. Also, the body messages as well as verbal messages of others can also promote or hurt the development of high self-efficacy.

Self-regulation has to do with the behavior that an individual sees as right or wrong and appropriate or inappropriate, followed by the resulting actions. The factors that influence self-regulation are being aware of what you are doing, judging the appropriateness of the behavior, and then deciding the necessary actions to take. In order to promote self-regulation, the individual should be taught to reward himself from time to time. An example might be that a child could watch a favorite television program after successfully completing a math assignment.
Self-instruction is a way of guiding behavior. It is therefore a strategy that is made up of conscious modeling combined with self-guidance.
Self-monitoring has to do with the observation of one's own behavior. Some individuals even grade themselves. It is a method by which one can control or change individual behavior.
Self-reinforcement is yet another method of controlling and/or changing one's behavior. It works by rewarding oneself or restricting a reward.

Discuss the principles of Maria Montessori's philosophy of learning, including multi-aged grouping, 3-hour work period, human tendencies, process of learning, indirect preparation, prepared environment and observation.

Discuss Carl Jung's theory regarding the basic ways that people deal with the world.

Discuss the philosophy of Montessori regarding schedule, assessment, requirements for ages 3–6, learning styles and character education.

Discuss the following principles of Montessori's philosophy of learning: work centers, method of teaching, class size, basic lessons, linking of study areas, and schedule.

Describe the scientific concepts that are age-appropriate for the Pre-K child.

Discuss letter knowledge and early word recognition. Then discuss the motivation to read.

Carl Jung developed the idea that people have four ways of dealing with their world. They are as follows:

Sensing: Information about the world is gathered through the senses, which is an act of perception instead of judgment; it is classified as irrational by Jung.

Thinking: Information is considered by making judgments, followed by decisions; it is classified as rational by Jung.

Intuiting: This is an internal type of perception in which a lot of information is integrated; it is classified as irrational by Jung.

Feeling: This is another form of information evaluation based on emotional responses; it is classified as rational by Jung.

Some of the principles of Montessori's philosophy of learning include:

Grouping of children should be by three-year age categories, such as 4–6.

The same teacher should stay with the group for all three years.

Curriculum should have its basis in exploration, moving around, making decisions, development of self-control, repetition, and development of abstract thinking through experimentation.

The process of learning begins with the introduction of an idea followed by processing and then understanding.

Children should always be learning something that prepares them for further learning. This results from teacher planning.

Teachers should provide many opportunities for the child to explore and create.

Teachers should observe and record the development and mastery of each child.

Additional principles of Montessori's philosophy of learning include:

The classroom is set up in learning centers through which the children may move at will. Also, there are no time limits at each center.

Textbooks are not used. Learning comes from other students and the environment.

A class of 30–35 children should have one teacher and one teaching assistant. The reasoning for this is that the class size can provide many different learning styles and personalities through which children learn from each other.

Individualized plans are developed for each child. This allows for the plans to be tailored to the child's readiness, ability and age.

The curriculum is based on the correlation of all areas of study.

The principles of Montessori include the following:

During the school day, one 3-hour block of time to work is present. This work period should not be interrupted.

Assessment is by the use of individual portfolios, and there are no grades, punishments, or rewards.

There are no requirements for ages 3–6. Children are just presented with large amounts of information.

All styles of learning, whether it be musical, natural, traditional or many others, are encouraged.

Many opportunities are provided for the development of values.

Knowledge regarding letters and their sounds is the key to beginning reading skills. The Pre-K child's skills that begin to develop are:

Understanding and connecting the names of letters to their shapes

Able to identify at least 10 letters

Noticing the beginning sounds of some words

Able to match letters with sounds

Able to read some frequently used words

Pre-K children need to have a classroom environment where reading is an enjoyable thing to do. Skills that show that the child is motivated to read include:

The child's body language indicates that he is interested in books.

He enjoys listening to stories.

He often asks that a story be reread.

He tries to read and write by himself.

Sharing books and pretending to read are common.

Visits to the library are enjoyable.

Some of the scientific concepts that are age-appropriate for the Pre-K child are as follows:

Properties of rocks, soil and water

Characteristics of living things

Changes in sound, weather, size and position

Knowledge that plants and animals are living things

Ability to group things according to living and nonliving

Understands the needs of living things

Identification of the materials from which objects are made

Develops the ability to use and understand patterns

Develops the ability to distinguish likenesses and differences

Ability to use scientific terminology to describe objects and events

Describe some of the skills regarding an understanding of history that are age-appropriate for the Pre-K child.

Describe some of skills regarding the individual, culture, and community that are age-appropriate for the Pre-K child.

Describe the development of skills as related to art, music, and drama in the Pre-K child.

Describe the skills that are age-appropriate for the Pre-K child as related to geography and economics.

Explain the importance to social and emotional development of positive environments in early life along with a nurturing relationship.

Describe the characteristics of physical movement, gross-motor development and fine-motor development in Pre-K children.

Skills that relate to the individual, culture, and community are as follows:
The child begins to share and to take turns with classmates and playmates.
The child develops a sense of cooperation.
He recognizes and can follow classroom rules.
He can perform certain jobs in the classroom and can make a contribution to the community of the classroom.
He is able to see likenesses and differences between himself and others.
He begins to develop the ability to see things from another's point of view.

The skills that are age-appropriate for the development of an understanding of history are as follows:
The Pre-K child is able to recognize simple events and routines such as story time.
He begins to develop an understanding of time such as tomorrow or yesterday.
He begins to develop an understanding of time as related to seasons and growth.
He begins to develop a connection between what happened yesterday and what happened today.
An understanding of cause and effect begins to develop.

The skills that are age-appropriate as related to geography are as follows:
Pre-K children are able to identify features such as the library in the school environment and the kitchen in the home environment.
Pre-K children are able to create drawings about their environment.
They begin to use words such as near and far.
They are able to identify features in their environment such as streets, houses, etc.
The skills that are age-appropriate as related to economics are as follows:
An understanding of the requirements or needs for all people
An understanding of what the community workers do
An understanding of the role of the consumer

The Pre-K child is able to:
Create art by using many materials
Create art by using different textures and shapes
Express himself through art
Share his art
Enjoy seeing others' art
Take part in musical activities in the classroom
Sing easy-to-remember songs
Start to play simple instruments
Begin to move to music
Act out stories or experiences
Create movement that displays feelings
Pretend-play with others
Distinguish between the sounds that different instruments make

The characteristics of physical movement include:
Movements in space
Relationship and names of body parts
Understanding boundaries
Running, jumping, hopping, and skipping
Movements in place such as bending
Participation in group games
The characteristics of gross-motor development include:
Ability to throw or kick in a given direction
Ability to catch large objects
Bouncing and catching a large ball
Better coordination of arms and legs

The characteristics of fine-motor development include:
Development of finger control when picking up things
Starting to button, zip, etc.
Beginning to hold pencils, crayons and pens with fingers
Ability to play with objects that have small parts
Beginning to use scissors for cutting

A healthy social and emotional development is encouraged when a child experiences the following:
Affection, attention, together with the care and interaction of the parent and other adults who provide care to the child
Cuddling and provision of needs
Stable emotional and social relationships of the adult caregivers
Environment rich in language-supporting activities
Sleeping environments that provide a quiet and restful place
Environments to play with toys that are appropriate for the age
Encouragement and support
Appropriate nutrition and safe living environment

List some of the physical developmental skills of three- and four-year-olds.

List some characteristics of children from 24 to 30 months and what activities can foster those skills. Then do the same for children from 30 to 36 months.

Explain how learning can be integrated across the curriculum by using a lesson on circles.

Discuss the important parts of planning and preparation of Pre-K lessons.

Explain the Montessori curriculum concept of early childhood education.

Explain how the use of a theme referred to as a "big idea" can help to organize curriculum.

Skill or Characteristic - 24–30 mo.	Activities by adults
Communicates with words	Should use words frequently
Plays with peers and teacher	Be supportive of the child's play
Shy when in a new situation	Help child to feel safe
Enjoys being with people	Play games with child
Smiles and laughs	Encourage imaginative activities
Likes books and games	Frequent reading of stories

Skill or Characteristic - 30–36 mo.	Activities by adults
Independent play	Encouragement
Can leave parents without distress	Provide help and encouragement
Demonstrates sharing	Provide help and praise
Begins to show empathy for others	Teach words for the feelings
Many emotions are expressed	Positive and consistent discipline
Likes books and games	Provide many activities for books

Physical developmental skills of three-year-olds are as follows:
Jumps on both feet in one place
Able to kick a ball
Able to ride a tricycle
Can swing if pushed
Able to build a tower of nine blocks
Can use scissors to snip
Uses three fingers to hold a crayon or pencil
Can imitate making a circle and a cross
Drawing of a person has only a head
Able to eat with a spoon and fork adequately
Physical developmental skills of four-year-olds are as follows:
Hops on one foot
Can play catch with a large ball
Able to build a tower of ten blocks
Able to make a string of beads
Can imitate making a square
Drawing of a person has a head and a body
Has an attention span of 30 minutes

Planning and preparation need to include the following decisions:
The lessons need to contain activities that will promote cross-curriculum learning.
Plan so that the lessons can correlate a child's experiences outside the classroom to the content that is being presented in the classroom.
Arrange and organize the classroom so that there are many opportunities to learn both intellectually and socially.
Make decisions as to what activities provide the best learning experiences for each child.
Plan your lessons creatively, and then be willing to make changes as needed.

Introduce the concept of circles by asking a riddle. Clues can be given that further describe circles. After identification of a circle has taken place, then discuss circular shapes that can be found in the classroom. All of the preceding activities build on the prior knowledge of the child. To prepare for a book reading, the teacher should show some of the pictures and start a discussion. During reading, actively involve the children by asking questions and getting responses from them. After the story, point out how the information fits into the real life of the child and then have them play a game about circles, such as finding as many examples of a circle as possible in a designated time frame. At the end of the game, record the results by putting the words of the items on a chart tablet. Then allow the children to draw pictures that will become part of a class book about circles.

Using a year-long theme can enable a teacher to organize a whole curriculum around one central idea or theme. This enables the child to link ideas together. It also provides structure and a basic vocabulary. An example of the "big idea" level of thematic instruction might be the theme Communities Share. At the beginning of the school year, the children learn that their classroom is a community, and that there are rules according to which the community lives, works, and plays. They start to learn to share with others in the classroom. This concept is enlarged to include the entire school, which can then be followed by neighborhoods and towns.

The Montessori curriculum concept is based on the complete differences between children and adults, specifically in the areas of developing and thinking. It is also strongly rooted in the idea of the rights of children. One of the principles of the Montessori curriculum is that there is no traditional measuring of achievement, such as tests or grades, because it damages the child's self-concept. Instead, the measurement is a portfolio displaying the achievements. Another principle is the importance of observing the child to discover his needs and characteristics. The focus is on the individual child's needs rather than the class. A great deal of independence is stressed along with the promotion of skills such as attention, eye-hand coordination, and completion of tasks.

Planning, Implementing, and Evaluating Instruction
© Mometrix Media - flashcardsecrets.com/praxisii
Pre-Kindergarten Education

Planning, Implementing, and Evaluating Instruction
© Mometrix Media - flashcardsecrets.com/praxisii
Pre-Kindergarten Education

Discuss the benefits of early childhood education.

Discuss the curriculum theory of Constance Kamii.

Planning, Implementing, and Evaluating Instruction
© Mometrix Media - flashcardsecrets.com/praxisii
Pre-Kindergarten Education

Planning, Implementing, and Evaluating Instruction
© Mometrix Media - flashcardsecrets.com/praxisii
Pre-Kindergarten Education

Discuss the findings of research on early childhood education.

List some characteristics of a quality early childhood education program.

Planning, Implementing, and Evaluating Instruction
© Mometrix Media - flashcardsecrets.com/praxisii
Pre-Kindergarten Education

Planning, Implementing, and Evaluating Instruction
© Mometrix Media - flashcardsecrets.com/praxisii
Pre-Kindergarten Education

Discuss the role of mental health practitioners in preschool assessment.

Discuss the characteristics of preschool assessment.

Constance Kamii studied under Piaget, who designed and developed the constructivist theory of education. This idea has to do with human beings constructing new knowledge from their own experiences. This process takes place through assimilation and accommodation. Assimilation has to do with the utilization of new experiences by putting them into what is already known. Accommodation is the process of learning through failure. The learner constructs the knowledge. Kamii believed that children should not be taught mathematics in the traditional way with formulas and algorithms such as borrowing, carrying and long division. Rather, she felt that children should learn through the discovery of their own methods to solve problems.

The greatest benefits of early childhood education can be seen in children who come from low socio-economic families and from families who lack education. Long-term benefits can be seen in lower drop-outs, fewer failures, better achievement scores, and decreased involvement in crime and delinquency. For these benefits to happen, however, the program must be of the highest quality. The quality is a result of the best staff, nurturing environments, helpful grouping, involvement of the parents, and consistent scheduling.

Some characteristics of a quality early childhood education program are as follows:
The environment is safe and nurturing.
The schedule is balanced between rest, play, and learning.
Meals and snacks are nutritious.
The curriculum has a strong language, literacy and math base.
A statement of goals and philosophy is present.
Teachers use lesson plans to develop activities with learning purposes.
Individual, small-group and large-group activities are equal.
Effective, regular communication with parents
Year-round, full day

Research has found the following items to be important components of effective Pre-K education:
Match resources and activities to developmental levels.
Raise the level of expectations.
Activities should flow from past experiences to exploration and discovery.
Provide a preview or introduction for every lesson.
New activities should be connected to many guided and independent practice experiences.
Monitor and provide assistance.
Provide an environment of caring.
Develop building of curriculum from each grade level.
Promote the development of skills for staff.
Promote parent involvement.

The use of criterion-referenced tests provides a method for individual testing of each child. No comparisons with other children are done. Rather, the comparisons are with developmental milestones. The settings for testing are designed to be relaxing and nonthreatening. One type of informal testing is referred to as Transdisciplinary Playbased Assessment, which was developed by Linder. While the child is playing with a person he knows, his actions are observed by a group of individuals. A child's disabilities are addressed by the development of assessments that provide accommodations for the disabilities. Assessments include multi-disciplinary, inter-disciplinary, and trans-disciplinary options.

The trend in preschool assessment is to have all of the persons who are involved with the child involved in the testing. Mental health practitioners are not necessarily directly involved in evaluation, but they provide helpful information to the family. Therefore, it is important for the mental health professionals to have a good understanding of the different types of assessment and to be able to explain to the family exactly the purpose of the tests and how they work. It is also part of their role to make sure that the assessment is conducted in the best environment possible for the child, that the testing instrument is matched to the needs of the child, and that the test administrators act in the most appropriate way for each child.

Discuss the typical layout of a preschool classroom.

Describe the environment of a preschool classroom.

Discuss the setup of the block center.

Discuss the setup of an art center.

Discuss the setup of the library center.

Discuss the setup of the dramatic play center.

A preschool classroom should encourage a child's curiosity and interest in his environment. It should be set up in a way that shows a child what is available to do and how to do these things. The classroom should also encourage interaction between the children. Normally, the preschool environment is built around learning centers. These are small areas that address different purposes. They provide a place for the child to play, explore, and learn. Preschoolers are at liberty to move freely from center to center. The centers are set up to develop and/or reinforce skills in the literacy, language, math, and other areas of learning, such as eye-hand coordination and development of fine and gross motor skills. The preschool centers that are usually included are literacy, dramatic play, manipulative, blocks, art, large motor, sensory, science, computer, and outdoor.

Even though a preschool classroom may seem to be a disorderly mass of small children moving around, it can be organized. Montessori's theory was that everything in the classroom should be matched to the size of the children. Everything should be low and comfortable. Some of the center areas would need to be larger than others. Some would need to be in parts of the room that are quieter. Everything should be labeled even though these children cannot read. Pictures of what the words mean can convey the concept that words carry meaning. When planning the classroom layout, the teacher needs to be sure that she can see what is going on in all areas even when she is working with the children in one area. Also, movement between areas needs to be unrestricted. Each center area's boundaries need to be identified with tape or shelves.

An art center should present many different types of art activities so that children have choices to make about what activity interests them. Place the materials in places that are easily reached by the children. Some of the materials that should be on hand are tempera paint (liquid of powder), paint brushes that have long handles, drop cloths for the floor, tables and easels, a drying rack, paper, pens, colored pencils, markers, newspapers, magazines, scissors, tape and glue. Old shirts can be used to protect clothing. Ask for materials such as cans, egg cartons, yarn, and many other materials from parents. Guidelines for the art center should include what to wear, what to do with the paintbrushes, what to do about spills, what to do when you are through, and how to interact with others while in the center.

The block center requires a lot of space. Many learning activities that develop skills such as communication, measurement, cooperation, problem solving and verbal development take place here. Make sure that crossing through the block center is not possible. Use rugs on the floor for comfort as well as noise curtailment. Blocks can be placed in containers on shelving that forms the boundaries. Label locations of the materials to facilitate cleanup time. Some guidelines for the block center should include maximum height of building. This would be no higher than the children's shoulder heights. Rules about knocking down others' projects need to be clear. Make sure that the children know what can be used to knock projects down and what to do when it is time to clean up.

The dramatic play center will be one of constant change, depending on the theme of study in the classroom. This will be a noisy center so it should be set up close to the block center. This is an area where social skills develop because it is where children interact with each other. Some of the materials that would be helpful to have are tables, chairs, dishes, blankets, dolls, kitchen furniture, telephones, dress-up clothes. Therefore, many storage containers will be required. Parents and thrift stores are good places to ask for materials. The teacher's role in the dramatic play center is more like a stagehand or prop person. At the beginning of the school year, it may be necessary for the teacher to initiate play in this center or to model play because the children may not know what to do.

The library center should be set up to encourage a love of books in children. It should be located in a quiet area of the classroom and does not have to be large. Baskets and shelves hold books. Large pillows can make it seem homey and comfortable. The library center can also serve as the computer center and a listening center for books on tape. Flannel board stories are another way of presenting literary works. The children would enjoy playing with the figures after the story. Some guidelines for the library center include turning pages carefully, rules for use of books (not throwing them, standing on them or writing in them), and what to do with the books when one is through.

Planning, Implementing, and Evaluating Instruction
© Mometrix Media - flashcardsecrets.com/praxisii
Pre-Kindergarten Education

Explain a good method of organization for classroom centers.

Planning, Implementing, and Evaluating Instruction
© Mometrix Media - flashcardsecrets.com/praxisii
Pre-Kindergarten Education

Discuss the setup of the manipulative center.

Planning, Implementing, and Evaluating Instruction
© Mometrix Media - flashcardsecrets.com/praxisii
Pre-Kindergarten Education

Discuss the behavior characteristics of a child who is a distracter in the classroom and how to handle the inappropriate behavior.

Planning, Implementing, and Evaluating Instruction
© Mometrix Media - flashcardsecrets.com/praxisii
Pre-Kindergarten Education

Describe the setup of the outdoor center.

Planning, Implementing, and Evaluating Instruction
© Mometrix Media - flashcardsecrets.com/praxisii
Pre-Kindergarten Education

Discuss the behavior characteristics of the child who is a dreamer and how to handle the inappropriate behavior.

Planning, Implementing, and Evaluating Instruction
© Mometrix Media - flashcardsecrets.com/praxisii
Pre-Kindergarten Education

Discuss the behavior characteristics of a child who is a goer in the classroom and how to handle the inappropriate behavior.

The manipulative center is also a math skill development center. Early writing skills are also developed here because of the fine motor skills that are used. Tables and chairs as well as carpet squares work for this center. Plastic tubs can be used to store the manipulatives. The skills that need to be developed are the determining factor for what materials are used. Some of the materials that can be made are file folder games, sewing cards, homemade puzzles, and homemade play dough. A good way to keep puzzle pieces together is to identically number all of the pieces that belong to the same puzzle.

It is an important part of classroom management to control the number of children that can be in a center at one time. One method is as follows: take a piece of corkboard about 3 feet wide and put picture names as well as the actual word names for each center on this board, which is attached to the wall. This is called an activity board. Then determine how many children can be at each center at a time. The number will be based on the total number of children and the total number of centers. An example based on a class of 15 with 7 centers would be:
Art - 3
Manipulatives - 3
Writing - 2
Library - 2
Science - 3
Blocks - 4
Dramatic Play – 4
Each child will have a name tag, which they may place using Velcro under the activity they want to go to first. When time is up for the first activity, they move to another center and move their name on the activity board.

The outdoor center should be designed for the development of large muscles. Also, the sand and water equipment can be moved to the outdoor center when the weather is nice. Other fair weather activities include sidewalk chalk art, gardening, finger painting, and clay sculpting. It is also important to set aside an area where the children can rest and have quiet play. Provide a basket of toys for this area. The teacher's role in this center is to be observant in order to prevent accidents. This center also provides a perfect environment to talk with the children about clouds, insects, plants, etc.

Some of the characteristics of a child who is a distracter in the classroom are as follows:
The child talks out and tries to get others to do the same.
The child has a short attention span.
The child interrupts classroom instruction.
The child does not pay attention and is easily distracted.
This misbehavior is usually caused by the student's need for attention. It could also be caused by failure to achieve or a struggle for power.
The teacher can try the following solutions:
Give the child responsibilities or jobs to perform.
Deal with the short attention span by shortening the length of an assignment.
Make contracts with the child or use the reward system to reinforce positive behavior.
Explain what the appropriate behavior looks like.
Consult with a counselor and alert the parents to a possible need for medical testing for an attention deficit.

Some of the characteristics of a child who is a goer in the classroom are as follows:
The child is constantly moving.
The child is constantly asking to go to the restroom or other ploys to not take care of the business at hand.
This behavior is usually caused by a child needing to be seen, or he may have a real physical problem. In this case, a medical doctor should be consulted.
The teacher can try the following solutions:
Set up some kind of structure for the moving about.
"No" does not always have to be the answer.
Set up time limits.
Always talk with the child privately.

The behavior characteristics of a child who is a dreamer are as follows:
The child's attention is not on what is going on in the classroom.
She is often engaged in some personal activity such as doodling.
She does not take part in the classroom discussion.
She is not aware that her behavior is not appropriate.
There are many possible causes for this type of inappropriate behavior. Some of them are lack of self-confidence, lack of proper nutrition, or living in a painful environment. Ways of dealing with this type of behavior are:
Do not constantly nag the child to pay attention.
Give the child one-on-one help and attention.
Conference with the parents.
Do not force the child to interact with others.
When there is success, reward in a private way.
Provide tasks the child can complete successfully.

Discuss the behavior characteristics of the child who is an attention demander and how to handle the inappropriate behavior.

Discuss the behavior characteristics of the child who is a do-nothing and how to handle the inappropriate behavior.

Discuss some keys to good classroom management.

Discuss ways that a preschool classroom can become a place to build community and encourage creativity.

Discuss what young children should learn in preschool.

Explain what a preschool learning environment looks like.

The behavior characteristics of a child who is a do-nothing are as follows:

Poor organization skills

Not a successful student even though the I.Q. may be high

Does not interact with the other children

Short attention span

Not neat

Some of the causes of this inappropriate behavior are lack of success or interest in classroom activities. The child also has low self-esteem caused by the pressure of parents and/or peers. As a result, he just does nothing. Some ways of dealing with this behavior are:

Conference with the parents.

Set up a verbal contract with the child.

Reinforce desired behavior in a positive manner.

Motivate the child by finding out his interests and using them.

Have the child work on only one activity at a time.

Monitor the child at all times.

Some of the behavior characteristics of the child who is an attention demander are as follows:

Extremely loud

Tries to join groups forcefully

Negative attitude toward authority

Has bully tendencies

Asks off-task questions

Some of the causes for this type of behavior are a need for attention, need to be part of a group, or lack of success. Ways to deal with this type of behavior are as follows:

Provide leadership situations for the child.

Double-up on responsibilities.

Provide appropriate ways to meet attention needs.

Be consistent, kind, and polite.

Model appropriate classroom behavior.

Reward by noticing desired behavior.

Exclusion is not appropriate.

First, the teacher must play the role of the coach on the sidelines. In this situation, learning becomes a celebration in which development is recognized and rewarded. The students live and learn in an atmosphere of community. There they develop cognitive, emotional and moral skills.

Many books and opportunities to use these books will promote the value of language. A safe environment is a must. If the students feel secure, they will be happier and learn more readily. Consistency provides a feeling of security. Access to computers makes learning exciting as well as enjoyable. It is important to develop a sense of community in the classroom, where leadership is shared. The stress should be on communication, reflection and reinforcement. Last, the teacher should model enthusiasm and activeness while he or she is being assertive.

One of the keys to good classroom management is setting up specific rules for the classroom at the very beginning. Then, follow up with reinforcement of the rules, reward students when the rules are followed, and consistently enforce consequences when the rules are not followed. The rules need to be specific about when talking is not appropriate and how to move in the classroom and other areas. It is also a good idea to have a limited number of rules. Present these rules at the beginning of the year. Then, review and reinforce on a daily basis. It is also valuable to engage the children in a discussion of the need for rules. When a child is breaking the rules, have him identify what rule is being broken and what he should have done instead.

A preschool learning environment includes opportunities for children to learn through social interaction with others. This learning is also a result of an interweaving of people, materials, tools, and symbols. The children have the opportunity to make decisions, explore, connect past learning experiences to the present, ask questions, and discover knowledge through experiences. The teacher becomes the guide in this environment. The children interact with the other children, the teacher, and the environment to explore, experience, and learn.

There are three principles that should be included in the preschool curriculum:

Learning should enable the child to understand the world he lives in. This learning should have its roots in the experiences from the past coupled with explorations that not only extend that learning but enrich it also.

Basic skills and knowledge in math, science and literacy need to be developed. Therefore, the curriculum should include opportunities to develop and practice the skills.

Problem-solving skills should be developed in the child by providing activities that are meaningful.

Discuss the Early Recognition Intervention Network (ERIN).

Explain some of the methods that teachers can use to develop mathematics and science skills in preschoolers.

Discuss the Montessori preschool curriculum model.

Discuss the High/Scope preschool approach curriculum model.

Discuss the Reggio Emilia curriculum model for preschool education.

Discuss the Project Approach preschool curriculum model.

First, preschool teachers can listen attentively to the students to discover their interests. It is important to plan activities that provide lessons based on the real world of the children. The teachers can ask open-ended questions that have to do with how, what, and why. Another strategy is to model experimentation. Giving feedback and providing structure for the learning activities are also good teaching strategies. The activities should encourage the development of skills and knowledge. Finally, it is important to remember that learning takes place in social relationships.

The principles upon which the Early Recognition Intervention Network (ERIN) is based are as follows:
This program is frequently used with special needs preschool children.
Materials and learning environment are organized to encourage and aid participation, body control, language skills, and visual perception.
Areas are set up around self-help, developmental skill promotion, and academic readiness.
Modifications of curriculum include physical space, time allotment, types of learning materials, organization of materials, method of grouping the children, and the use of cues by the teachers.

The High/Scope preschool approach model is based upon the following principles:
- Children learn best when they can help plan, implement, and look back on what they observed.
- There are 58 key identifiers or experiences for child development during preschool.
- The 58 key experiences are grouped into ten categories: creative play, language/literacy, social relationships, movement, music, classification, seriation, numbers, space and time.
- Most of the activities of a typical day in the classroom follow the "plan, do, review" basis.
- The activities are carried out both in large and small group settings, which include outside experiences.

The Montessori preschool curriculum model is based on the following principles:
- Children learn by experiencing.
- The environment needs to be structured.
- Materials are both informative and sequential.
- Curriculum is based in development of the senses, academic development, real life competence, and moral development.
- Two thirds of the class day is spent in activities that are independent.
This model was the first to be widely accepted and copied.

The Project Approach preschool curriculum model is based on using projects to find out more information about a specific subject. It is not intended to look for answers to questions devised by the teacher but rather to look for answers to things that the children want to find out. This does not make up the entire preschool curriculum. It covers only an informal part and is usually developed around themes or topics chosen by the teacher.

The Reggio Emilia curriculum is based on the interests of the children and developed by the teacher. Parents and community support is included. It is referred to as an emergent curriculum. The graphic arts are integrated into learning and used to develop cognitive, language, and social development. This is referred to as representational development. The curriculum also uses collaborative group work. Through this type of learning the children learn to use language to critique and compare as well as to negotiate and solve problems. The teacher's role is to be a facilitator and provider of materials. Children's progress is documented by using portfolios. The classroom environment is important because it is essential to learning.

Define curriculum and curriculum model.

Discuss the theme-based model of preschool curriculum.

Explain Title III of the Americans with Disabilities Act.

Explain the meaning of Title I.

Explain the purpose of preschool under Title I.

Explain the meaning of preschool as connected to Title I.

The theme-based model of preschool curriculum is based on the following principles:

- Themes often are results of the environment of the children.
- There are many different ways to explore a theme.
- A theme should have some relationship to daily experiences in the classroom.
- It is important to include the children in the planning phase.
- Cross-curriculum learning should be incorporated into the theme.
- New learning should be stressed.
- Needs of the children should be taken into consideration.

Curriculum is the total program of education. It includes everything from the daily activities and routines that affect physical, social, emotional and cognitive development of children.

A **curriculum model** is a system that is a combination of both practice and theory in an educational setting. It is usually supported by research. The model includes instructions about how to set up the physical environment along with specific activities to use. It also suggests methods to involve parents and other family members. When a curriculum model is chosen, be sure that it is consistent with research.

Title I is a part of the Elementary and Secondary Education Act of 1965. Its purpose is to ensure that all children have an equal chance for a quality education. This can be accomplished if the following takes place:

- A system of accountability is in place along with quality preparation of teachers and assessment tools.
- The needs of low-income, migratory, disabled, Native American, limited English, and/or neglected children are met.
- The gap between the performance of minority and disadvantaged children and the others is minimized.
- Schools are held accountable for performance of all children.
- Schools are provided with resources.
- State-wide assessment systems are used.
- Individual schools are given greater power to make decisions.
- More quality instruction time is provided.
- The quality of instruction improves.
- Services with other agencies are coordinated.
- There are many opportunities for parental involvement.

The basic requirements of Title III of the Americans with Disabilities Act are as follows:

A. Teachers or childcare providers may not discriminate against a child on the basis of disability alone. In other words, services must be provided to the child unless one of the following conditions is present:

1. The child is a threat to the health or safety of others.
2. Making the necessary modifications for the child would present a major change.
3. Providing communication aids and services would create an undeserved financial load.

B. The facilities must be made accessible to individuals with disabilities. If the facility is not new, then changes must be made. If the facility is being built, then the accommodations must be included. The act states the accommodations must be "fully accessible."

Preschool means educational programs for children who qualify and are of the age for which the local educational agency provides instruction. The purpose of preschool is to provide development of skills that will raise the level of achievement for these children once they do reach school age. Any child from birth to school age (the age at which free education is provided by the local education agency (LEA)) may attend preschool.

The purpose of preschool under Title I is to provide experiences that will help children meet the educational standards necessary to be successful throughout their school years. Research has shown that disadvantaged children are several years behind in normal developmental skills. Title I seeks to eliminate this disability for these children. Part of the statutes in the ESEA requires local educational agencies to provide the best programs available for the economic disadvantaged as early as possible. If the gap is closed, these children have a much better chance at being successful in school. The benefits include better performance in math and reading, less retention, less chance of being in special education, fewer discipline problems, better attendance, and more enthusiasm toward education.

Explain the nature of activities that occur during a typical preschool day.

List some of the components of a successful preschool program.

Discuss other instructional strategies of a preschool teacher.

Describe the nature of instruction during a preschool day.

Discuss professional development for preschool teachers.

Discuss how preschool teachers can monitor the progress of the children in an effective manner.

Some of the components of a successful preschool program include:

- Goal and mission statement are comprehensive in nature and specific in how the program will work.
- The activities that the children are engaged in are meaningful.
- Curriculum is based on the development of skills necessary for success in kindergarten.
- Instruction is planned and an equal amount of time is spent in large and small groups.
- There is a secure and warm environment that nurtures literacy.
- There is frequent monitoring of progress.
- There is frequent communication with parents.
- There are intensive time allotments.

Some of the activities that occur in a preschool classroom are seen as blocks of time. Each block focuses on special learning areas. Some of the blocks will be guided learning provided by the teacher. Others will be times of search and find. Often the block will simply be a time when the child can practice skills he has already learned. All of the preschool day should be used for some type of learning experience for the child. Some of the experiences resemble play, but children learn through play. Also, all types of skills can be taught in one activity.

The most important thing for preschool teachers to remember is that learning should address all of the developmental areas of a child. These include social, emotional, language, physical, and intellectual areas. However, many skills in one area will develop through activities in another area. Learning to some degree will take place naturally as children interact with their environment and others. However, some skills have to be taught. Research has shown that a good teaching strategy is to build new learning on the past experiences (or what the child already knows). For example, success in reading is dependent on early sound awareness and vocabulary-building activities in preschool.

Preschool teachers can help children to develop listening and speaking skills by asking open-ended questions, exposing them to new words, allowing the children to take part in conversations, and being warm and encouraging. Reading aloud to children is important because it is here that they learn about printed words and their meanings. Another strategy for language and literacy development is to share books with a child. Providing many opportunities to hear the sounds of words develops reading readiness. This can be done through playing games and listening to books being read. Young children should have many opportunities to explore their environment and to learn about the world. Through these activities language is developed and problem-solving skills are learned.

Preschool teachers can monitor the progress of the children in many different ways. The progress needs to cover academic, social, and emotional development. Monitoring progress is important because it helps the teacher plan instruction and also be sure all of the needs of the child are being addressed. This can be done by:

- Observing the child while he plays and interacts with others
- Keeping samples of his work
- Making sure that progress is documented
- Conversing with the child about his progress
- Conversing with the parents to find out what they have seen at home

The most important part of the preschool teacher's job is to implement the curriculum by using instructional strategies that are effective. Therefore, because the child is so influenced by the interactions with the teacher, it is even more critical for that teacher to have professional development. This professional development should cover ways to support and expand a child's cognitive and language skills. Training should be on research-proven topics such as child development, literacy, assessment, and acquisition of language. Mentoring and coaching are also helpful topics for professional development.

Explain methods to make the transition from preschool to kindergarten easier.

Discuss way to engage parents in preschool education.

Explain the No Child Left Behind Act of 2001.

Explain the importance of parent involvement in preschool.

Explain the Head Start program.

Explain the Improving America's Schools Act (IASA) of 1994.

Family environments in which the parents take part in activities that are rich in language and interaction with the child provide strong foundations for literacy and intellectual development. Environments in which the child is read to, and the family stresses the importance of learning also strengthen this foundation. The teacher's role is to share as much information about the child's development as possible with the parents. The teacher should meet with them to share information about what topics are being covered at school and any difficulties that may be present. These meetings do not have to be formal. A few words with the parent when they are picking up or dropping the child off can be helpful. Another way to communicate with parents is through newsletters.

There are several methods to make the transition from preschool to kindergarten easier. One is to make sure that the goals and curriculum are aligned in both preschool and kindergarten. This can be promoted by providing professional development for these teachers together. Another method is to have both levels visit each other's classrooms. Another method is providing the kindergarten teacher with a portfolio of the preschool child's work. Communication is the best way to make the transition easier. It is helpful when the preschool teacher can share any information about the child that might not show up in the portfolio. The best way to do this is through the use of documentation of what has been done in the past to help and what the result may have been.

It is of utmost importance to the future of the child to have parents who are involved in his or her education. Sometimes it is the school's role to educate or train the parents in methods whereby they can help their child at home. Research has shown that the children who have supportive parents are much more successful at school. As a matter of fact, there is a direct correlation between achievement of the child and the amount of family engagement in the preschool program. This research has shown that all children, no matter what background or income level, have higher achievement with parental involvement.

This act, known as the NCLB, has the following characteristics:
- It is designed to improve the performance of schools.
- It increases standards of accountability.
- It gives parents greater freedom to choose the schools their children will attend.
- It targets reading skills as a high priority.
- It sets high goals and expectations for students.
- It gives each student's name, address, and phone number to recruiters from the military.

The Improving America's Schools Act came to life during the Clinton administration. It provided for the following:
- The Title I program, which helped disadvantaged children
- Charter schools, autonomous public schools that are supposed to use innovative methods to produce outstanding results
- Technology
- Bilingual and migrant education
- Safe and drug-free schools
- Impact aid, a method of federal financial assistance for certain qualifying school districts
- Eisenhower Professional Development

The Head Start program's purpose is to help children be more ready for school by providing educational, health, nutritional, and social services through grants to public and private nonprofit agencies. These grants help agencies provide many services to the children of economically disadvantaged families. The emphasis educationally is to promote early reading and math skills, which will give these children a "head start" when they start kindergarten or first grade. It is designed for children from birth to three years. The parents of these children also receive training to help them achieve their educational, employment, and literacy goals.

Explain the eight elements of multiple intelligences.

Discuss learning modalities (styles).

Discuss the various teaching techniques that promote the different learning modalities.

Explain the methods that can be used to determine the best individual learning styles.

Discuss learning through sensory-motor integration.

Discuss the three basic learning styles.

Learning modalities refer to the way children and adults learn. Some theorists refer to only three—visual, motor, and auditory. A visual learner learns from watching lessons being modeled. They are also able to learn from pictures in books. Many times, these children are easily distracted by other activities going on in the classroom. Children who learn from motor activities need to be involved in the actual "hands-on" learning experiences. This type of learning is also referred to as kinesthetic. Auditory learners most often learn by hearing and being told what to do. They, too, are distracted by background noise. These modalities refer to the way that the child processes and retains information. Often, a child will demonstrate combinations of these learning styles. The term multiple intelligences refers to the potential inherited biological traits that can be influenced by education and culture.

The elements of multiple intelligences that provide more distinguishable characteristics of learning modalities are:

- **Linguistic/Language**: learning takes place through reading, listening to the teacher, oral discussions, playing games with words
- **Logical/Mathematics**: abstract thinking and exploration are characteristics
- **Spatial**: enjoys models, drawing, puzzles, maps, and videos
- **Musical**: learning takes place through songs and rhymes; enjoys musical instruments
- **Bodily kinesthetic**: learns by touch and manipulation; likes to build
- **Interpersonal**: social and outgoing; learns through group interactions
- **Intrapersonal**: independent worker; self-motivated; requires quiet environment
- **Naturalist**: scientific learner; interested in nature and the environment; asks questions

Discovering learning styles for individual children requires a great deal of observation, but no tests. Document the behavior of the children. They can be sorted according to the elements of multiple intelligences or simply a determination of which style the child learns the best with. Some questions or actions that should be noted during observation are things like: what activities do the children enjoy most; does the child like to watch a lesson or to be told about something; does the child like to experiment; what do they spend their spare time doing; do they work independently or in groups; what computer games do they choose when given a choice.

The classroom should be set up with many different types of centers that address the different learning modalities. Look at these centers with the idea of determining how many modalities each one addresses. Plan different activities that use different modalities to teach the same concepts. An example for teaching a group of new words might be (1) teacher writes the words on the board and points them out (auditory and visual); (2) children sing the words to a familiar song (musical); (3) the children then write the words in a journal (motor/kinesthetic); and the lesson ends with another song where the children point to the words. Teaching a theme-based lesson that has high interest for the children is another good technique. Then, all phases of the curriculum can be pulled into the learning.

Children have a preferred, or more natural way of learning, but they can learn through any one of the three learning styles. It is important that the parent and teacher are aware of their own learning styles so that they can be sure to teach in the learning style by which the child learns best. Encouragement of the child to develop all three styles is important. One idea is to let him use the preferred style when learning new material, and then to let him use any of the other styles when the topic is not as important. Very young children are almost always kinesthetic learners. As the child grows older, learning may become more difficult if he does not development the other learning styles. An important key to promoting learning is to make the experience enjoyable.

Sensory-motor integration is a cycle of brain development that occurs between three and seven. It is a time when whole picture concepts begin to develop. Other skills that are developed during these years are cognition, imagery, rhythm, speech, emotions, and intuition. Playground equipment helps develop the nervous system as well as sensory integration. Using scissors, knives, forks, and spoons develops fine motor skills. Young girls will make up games to express their newly developed skills while boys will demonstrate displays of strength.

Some possible "red flags" for these development skills are:

- The child cannot distinguish colors.
- She cannot solve puzzles.
- C. He cannot identify a written name.
- D. She does not respond to directions quickly.
- E. Nursery rhymes are learned slowly.
- F. He is not attentive to stories.
- G. Attention span is poor.
- H. Social development is poor.
- The child has difficulties with sleeping and eating.
- J. He is slow to toilet train.
- K. She does not demonstrate a dominant hand

Discuss the sensory experience and movement.

Explain sensory integration.

Explain the Americans with Disabilities Act of 1992 and the No Child Left Behind Act of 2001.

Explain the 1986 Amendments to the Education for All Handicapped Children Act, Individuals with Disabilities Education Act of 1992, and Amendments to the Individuals with Disabilities Education Act of 1997.

Explain Section 504 of the Rehabilitation Act and the Elementary and Secondary School Act.

Explain the Individuals with Disabilities Education Improvement Act of 2004.

Sensory integration is the ability to use information from the senses as a basis for learning. Children learn by interacting with their environment. This interaction is directed by the senses. Information from the senses should flow in an integrated manner. The brain can then take this information and form perceptions along with behavior and learning. If no integration takes place, then this information cannot be used. The perceptual functions that are basic for young children are visual, auditory, and tactile discrimination. Sensations are guided by prior sensory experiences and to what extent the child is affected. A light touch to one child might be perceived as something painful to another.

Vision is one of the most important sensory experiences that affect learning. Most sensory input is visual. Many of the nerve endings to muscles are connected to motor nerves in the eyes. Hearing is also important. Movement of the head is directly connected to identification of sound. If a child cannot hear properly due to possible multiple ear infections, normal development of movement can be delayed. Also, the ability to process information is blocked. This may result in a developmental delay in language (written and spoken). Sensory input must follow a particular sequence. All of the skills must be addressed. Otherwise, the development is lacking, which can cause learning difficulties.

1986 Amendments to the Education for All Handicapped Children Act:
- This act enlarges the coverage to include preschool children who have disabilities.
- It mandates that every school district must conduct a multidisciplinary assessment and develop a family service plan for each preschool age child with disabilities.

Individuals with Disabilities Education Act of 1990:
- This reauthorizes the Education for All Handicapped Children Act.
- Traumatic brain injury and autism are added to the list of disabilities.
- Transition services are defined.
- Assistive technology is made readily available.

Amendments to the Individuals with Disabilities Education Act of 1997:
- This clarifies who will be participants on the IEP teams as well as IEP documentation.
- IDEA changes include disciplinary issues.
- Requirements are extended to state reports regarding the performance and progress of the total enrollment of students.

The Americans with Disabilities Act of 1992:
Persons with disabilities cannot be discriminated against in:
- employment
- places of public accommodation
- places of public transportation
- telecommunication services

No Child Left Behind Act of 2001:
- Elementary and Secondary Education Act is reauthorized.
- The provisions of the ESEA Act include all students.
- It requires reading and math assessments each year (grades 3–8) plus one year in high school.
- It requires interventions related to literacy up through Reading First and Early Reading First.
- Parents are given more freedom to change schools or districts when the school's performance is not up to par.

The Individuals with Disabilities Education Improvement Act of 2004:
- Teachers who teach students with disabilities must have special education certification or pass a licensing exam.
- It establishes new identification methods for the learning disabled.
- Discrepancy scores are not required.
- 15% of special education funds may be used for students who have not yet been identified.
- Teachers must be special education certified and core subject certified if they teach to alternate achievement standards in core subjects.
- IEPs no longer need benchmarks and short-term objectives.
- Multi-year IEPs may be allowed.
- Transition planning must be based on results goals.
- Parent surrogates must be appointed if a disabled child is homeless or a ward of the court.

Section 504 of the Rehabilitation Act:
This act prohibits discrimination against people because they have a disability. Furthermore, federal money can be taken away from any entity that is guilty of discrimination. Discrimination includes excluding anyone from participating in or getting benefits from any program that receives federal money. Of course, the individual must be qualified. The exclusion is referring to exclusion based only on the disability.

Elementary and Secondary School Act of 1965:
- This act was designed to help provide for the educational needs of poor people.
- Preschool was included in the needs list.
- Head Start schools were a result of ESEA.
- Follow-Through was another program that was designed to continue the work started in Head Start.
- Bi-lingual education targeted Spanish-speaking children.
- ESEA also included many counseling and guidance programs for these children.

Discuss other issues regarding disabilities according to Title III.

Discuss some of the issues regarding specific disabilities according to Title III.

Describe the specific duties required of a preschool teacher.

List other guidelines of Title III.

Explain the licensing requirements for preschool teachers.

Describe some of the positive traits required of a preschool teacher.

Children with HIV or AIDS: These children cannot be excluded according to Title III. Necessary precautions such as rubber gloves and contact with body fluids need to be taken.

Children who are mentally retarded: These children may not be excluded according to Title III. They should be integrated into all the activities that the other children are engaged in. They may not be segregated.

Children with life-threatening allergies to insect stings and foods: These children cannot be excluded based on their allergies. The necessary supplies and steps to take in the event of a reaction need to be in place.

Children with diabetes: These children cannot be excluded. The necessary supplies and steps to take in the event of a diabetic incident need to be in place.

Children with mobility impairments: If these children need assistance in removing leg braces, etc., this assistance should be provided. The only exclusion might be if the device was so complicated that it required a health care professional, or if the other children would be neglected when the child was cared for.

Children who are deaf: Auxiliary aids and services must be provided unless it would prove to be an extreme financial burden.

Children who hit and bite others: if all steps have been taken to stop the threatening behavior, the child (even with disabilities) can be expelled from the school.

Children with seeing-eye dogs: the service dog must be allowed to accompany the child; this is true even if there is a "no pet" policy.

Children who are developmentally delayed: These children must be accepted and placed in a classroom with the peers (age).

No additional charges may be made for a child with disabilities. If there were medical necessities that the school did not have, it would not be required to furnish these services. Simple procedures would have to be provided at no extra charge, however.

A school normally may not refuse to give a child with disabilities medication. Instructions along with reasonable care should protect the school from any liability.

A school cannot refuse to diaper a child who wears diapers due to a disability. If a child needs additional help due to the disability in getting to the restroom, this service too must be provided.

Some of the specific duties required of a preschool teacher include:
- Preparation of daily lesson plans; these need to be based on learning basic skills.
- Planning of creative activities; keep in mind the imagination of the children.
- Preparation and planning of outdoor activities; these should be based on motor skill development.
- Make sure that the outside and inside environments are safe for the children.
- Take care of the basic needs of the children such as food and bathroom needs.
- Provide comfort and nurturing.
- Monitor and assess development of skills.
- Meet with parents as well as other professional educators.
- Be able to communicate goals and methods of improvement.

Some of the positive traits required of preschool teachers include:
- **Compassion**: the children need to feel safe and cared for; creates a good learning environment.
- **Communicate effectively with the children**: children can understand what is being said; confusion is not an issue.
- **Good people skills**: can communicate easily with the children and others; able to relate to children as well as adults.
- **Alert**: know what is going on in the classroom at all times; know where the children are.
- **Good planner**: be adept at constructing interesting and challenging plans; plans should meet the goals.
- **Creative**: be able to plan creative activities.

Each state has different licensing requirements for preschool teachers. A state license to teach in public schools is more exacting than one for teaching in private schools. Normally, states require a bachelor's degree in early childhood education for a public school certification. There is also a type of certification called the Child Development Associate (CDA), which involves a combination of experience working with children, assessment of competence plus classroom education. Private schools do not have any state mandates; however, they prefer to hire individuals with the same credentials as required by the state. Furthermore, if the school is governed by a church, the school normally wants individuals with the same value base as the church.

Discuss the learning environment of preschool children.

Discuss other requirements that are necessary for a successful preschool teacher. List the other opportunities in the educational field for preschool teachers with more training.

Explain the 1986 Amendment to P.L. 94-142 (EHA) and the 1990 Amendment P.L. 101-476 regarding preschool programs.

Discuss the use of computers in a preschool classroom.

Explain the Circle of Inclusion model.

Discuss the characteristics (ethnicity and poverty status) of children in preschool programs.

Some of the other requirements that are necessary for one to be a successful preschool teacher are as follows:

- Must know material to be taught
- Be able to communicate and express oneself
- Create an atmosphere of trust
- Be able to help students want to learn
- Should be knowledgeable about child development and the needs of children
- Should be knowledgeable about differences between cultures
- Have a cooperative nature
- Be organized and dependable
- Have a patient nature
- Be creative in planning activities

If a preschool teacher receives additional education and training, there are other employment opportunities in the educational setting. Being a school librarian, counselor, or a reading specialist are a few. Also, there are opportunities to become administrators or supervisors. It is also possible for a preschool teacher to work her way up in the system, which would involve being an assistant to start with, and possibly ending up as a lead teacher.

Play and activities where children interact with others or with things are the main ways a preschool child learns. A good teacher can make good use of this play to encourage language development. Some activities that aid this learning are storytelling and games that use rhymes or drama. Another "plus" of learning through play activities is social development. Certain math and science skills can also be taught using play activities. Other methods of teaching include small group activities and one-on-one teaching. Art, music, and drama are exceptional tools for this age because the children have a natural love for them. Certainly some academic skills are taught at the preschool level, such as recognition of letters and numbers, sounds that letters make, and an awareness of the world.

Computers are becoming an important part of any classroom regardless of the age of the children. There are many different types of software available, and the use of computers is a great interactive way to present learning. Children are able to communicate with others in faraway places. Some of the games are just another way of learning and practicing skills that they have learned in another setting. Children have a natural curiosity about computers. English can even be taught to non-English-speaking children, plus other languages can be taught to English-speaking children. Not only are computers a good learning tool for the children, but they are also a great help for the teacher. Computers can be used to make worksheets as well as record grades and communicate with other teachers and parents.

The 1986 amendment to the EHA regarding preschool programs is as follows:

- The age requirement for the provision of a free and appropriate education for children with disabilities was extended to include those children ages 3–5.
- Early intervention programs had to be developed for children with disabilities during ages 0–2.
- Individual family service plans had to be developed for every family who had an infant or toddler with a disability.

The 1990 amendment to the EHA includes the following:

- The name "EHA" was changed to Individuals with Disabilities Education Act (IDEA).
- The phrase "handicapped child" was changed to "child with disabilities."
- Brain injury and autism were added to the list of disabilities.
- The IEP must include assistive technology devices and services.
- Least restrictive environment was extended to mean in a classroom with children who do not have disabilities and at the age appropriate level.
- Children must be transitioned by age 16.

Preschool programs include Head Start, pre-kindergarten, nursery school, and daycare centers. About 57% of children ages 3–5 in the U.S. attend some kind of preschool program. Forty-seven percent of these children are from poor families. More black and white children are enrolled in preschool programs than Hispanic. Only 43% of Hispanic children attend as compared to 59% white and 66% black. Another statistic is that a great deal more children attend whose mothers had post-graduate high school education than those who did not finish high school. Seventy-three percent of the children attending have mothers who have a bachelor's degree or higher education.

The features of the Circle of Inclusion model include:

- Values and vision of inclusion in an early childhood education are shared.
- Placements for children with disabilities are held in preschool programs that are high quality.
- There are links to childcare services for children with disabilities.
- Opportunities to learn are provided for children with disabilities in a child-centered environment.
- Facilitators are provided in classroom settings for the child with disabilities.
- Classrooms have a natural proportion of children with disabilities.
- Teams are set up that meet on a routine basis to assess the needs and progress of each disabled child.
- Special education personnel work on an integrated team approach.
- In-service programs are provided to all staff on an ongoing basis.
- Decisions are based on input from family as well as staff.
- The goals and outcomes of the program are clearly stated.

Explain the barriers to preschool inclusion programs.

Explain the values of the Circle of Inclusion model.

Discuss Howard Gardner's eight elements of multiple intelligences.

Discuss the meaning and application of learning modalities.

Discuss the establishment of individual support in the positive behavior support model.

Discuss positive behavior support.

The values of the Circle of Inclusion model include:
- Children with disabilities should not have to meet certain requirements before they can be admitted to a preschool program.
- Disabled children and children with normal development should be able to get to know each other and to interact.
- Everyone involved in an inclusion model should work collaboratively.
- Every child should be respected as an individual.
- Inclusive programs should use the best approaches to learning available as well as age-appropriate materials.
- Makeup of individuals in a classroom should be based on normal proportions.
- Variables that promote success should be explored.

Some of the barriers to a successful preschool inclusion program include:
- Many times the personnel do not have the necessary training to teach children with disabilities.
- There are different views of preschool education and special ed preschool education. Each one has a special way of educating the child.
- Many of the services that a child with disabilities might need are not normally part of an early childhood program.
- Lack of monitoring systems cause uncertainty about who is responsible for what in the inclusion programs.
- Many attitudes of adults act as roadblocks for inclusion programs. These include everything from parents protecting the child from what they perceive as possible threats to their self-esteem to teachers who feel they are not qualified to teach disabled children.

There are several different ways of referring to learning modalities. They are also called learning styles as well as multiple intelligences. They all have to do with the way people, including children, learn best. Furthermore, often people learn from combinations of these modalities. Everyone is different. For the most part, learning modalities are classified into three categories—visual, motor and auditory. Learning modalities or styles are a combination of ways in which people concentrate, process, and store information. A person's ability to learn is based in genetics, and the influences of education and culture are usually thought of as multiple intelligences.

Howard Gardner's eight elements of multiple intelligences are as follows:
Linguistic (language): learns through activities related to language such as reading, verbalization, and listening. These children enjoy games related to words, reading and listening to books, poetry, and songs.
Logical (mathematical): thinks in abstract patterns, is able to reason, enjoys performing tests.
Musical: learns through the rhythm of music. These children enjoy playing instruments and singing.
Spatial: learns best through solving puzzles, designing and building and working with charts, maps and diagrams.
Bodily kinesthetic: learns best through body experiences such as touching and manipulating objects.
Interpersonal: Learns best through socialization with others and group activities.
Intrapersonal: is an independent learner; enjoys and learns best in quiet environments.
Naturalist: learns best when working with scientific investigation.

Positive behavior support is an approach to discipline where children are taught social and communication skills in surroundings that are built around learning. It involves approaches that are a combination of problem solving, new skills, systems that are changing, and positive support. In addition, positive behavior support is the same for all children at the school plus a group level for the children who need more support. Finally, there is an individual support system for those children who have severe behavior problems.
In setting up the universal support, present the children with a set of rules and expectations. Then, reward consistently for the following of these rules and expectations. Next, set up the group support, which will govern activities in the classroom and other places such as the hallway, playground, or cafeteria. Consistently reinforce and reward.

The individual support part of the positive behavior support model is designed for the children who have more severe behavior problems. First, a functional assessment needs to be completed so that the reasons for the inappropriate behavior can be determined. This functional assessment should include an identification of what is going on immediately before the problem behavior as well as immediately after. It can also supply important information about teacher responses and information as to what can be done to prevent this behavior from occurring in the future. The most important thing for teachers to remember is to be proactive with these children. This means trying to head off situations that are known to trigger behavioral problems. Also, the child can be taught how to use skills to help himself when encountering problem situations.

Discuss some effective proactive strategies that can be used to prevent problem behavior in the classroom.

Discuss strategies for teachers who have behavior problems in their classroom.

Explain some methods to adapt instructional strategies.

Explain how a teacher should effectively deal with parental concerns regarding discipline problems with disabled children in the classroom.

Discuss the integration of the internet and use of computers into the early childhood classroom.

Explain methods of adapting instructional materials.

First, teachers who have behavior problems in their classroom should determine what causes the problem behavior. Then, they should come up with a plan to prevent the behavior. Children many times cannot express what they need, which becomes a behavior problem. These needs may involve trying to avoid something such as performing the required tasks at school. They could also be connected to desires to get something like attention, or they can even be caused by a medical problem. If a teacher knows why the child is acting out, she can better deal with the behavior. The idea is to positively reinforce desired behavior patterns.

Some effective proactive strategies that a teacher can use to prevent problem behavior in the classroom are as follows:

- Teach and direct a child toward desired methods of behavior instead of reinforcing the inappropriate behavior.
- Prompt and reinforce the behavior that is desired during time periods when the child has been most likely to exhibit the inappropriate behavior.
- Mix up easy tasks with difficult tasks if inappropriate behavior has been occurring when the tasks become difficult for the child.
- Set up a schedule that has consistent as well as predictable patterns of transition.
- Help children to manage their own behavior by monitoring successful efforts.

The most important thing for a teacher to do when dealing with any child, disabled or not, who has disruptive behavior is to prevent that child from hurting others and to respond in a concerned manner to the parents. First, the teacher needs to be aware of the rights of all children to a good education and to be able to explain these rights to the concerned parents. IDEA (Individuals with Disabilities Act) states that children who have disabilities must be educated with those who do not. It also mandates that if a child's disruptive behavior hurts his own learning or that of others, then positive intervention steps should be taken to stop the disruptive behavior. All teachers should have a plan in place to deal with potentially harmful behavior from any child in their classroom.

Adapting instructional strategies refers to ways that a teacher can change the way she presents information. One strategy is to use demonstrations and role playing. Use presentation cues such as visual or verbal emphasis. This could also include gesturing. Another strategy is to actively engage the children in the learning process. The activity where children respond to statements or questions with "thumbs up-thumbs down" is a good way to get them involved. The use of manipulatives is another strategy that works well with children who learn well with motor activities. Then, modify the way instruction is delivered by varying large group/small group instruction as well as independent work with guided work.

When instructional materials are adapted, the child has access to these materials during the learning process. This is a way of changing the supplies that a child has so that he can experience learning through a number of different modalities. Design these materials so that they reach all of the senses and not just the visual and auditory. Present curriculum through the use of models, graphics, pictures, or digitized forms. Select instructional materials that are designed for the safety of the children. Also, select materials that are durable and will last through much use. Paper text (books, etc.) can be laminated. Plastic should be chosen over glass. Soft books are another adaptive material.

Teachers can use the internet with young children to enhance learning that is being presented in the classroom. This use can foster experimentation and exploration as well as the development of problem-solving skills. Computers can also be used as a means to practice math and emerging literacy skills in yet another modality. Math skills such as sequencing, patterns, and number relationships can be practiced online. Letter recognition and word/picture relationships are also available. Creativity can be developed by writing tools, which can be used on computers. These activities need to be correlated with learning experiences in the real world also. There are many ways that the internet can be used to provide experiences along a theme-based lesson.

Planning, Implementing, and Evaluating Instruction
© Mometrix Media - flashcardsecrets.com/praxisii
Pre-Kindergarten Education

Explain methods to provide internet safeguards in the early childhood classroom.

Planning, Implementing, and Evaluating Instruction
© Mometrix Media - flashcardsecrets.com/praxisii
Pre-Kindergarten Education

Discuss the evaluation of appropriate websites for the early childhood classroom.

Planning, Implementing, and Evaluating Instruction
© Mometrix Media - flashcardsecrets.com/praxisii
Pre-Kindergarten Education

Explain the importance of dramatic play in the early childhood classroom.

Planning, Implementing, and Evaluating Instruction
© Mometrix Media - flashcardsecrets.com/praxisii
Pre-Kindergarten Education

Discuss ways to foster visualization of curriculum content.

Planning, Implementing, and Evaluating Instruction
© Mometrix Media - flashcardsecrets.com/praxisii
Pre-Kindergarten Education

Discuss the setting up of centers in the early childhood classroom.

Planning, Implementing, and Evaluating Instruction
© Mometrix Media - flashcardsecrets.com/praxisii
Pre-Kindergarten Education

Explain the creation of sociodramatic play boxes.

The educational goals along with the age of the children are the determining factors for choosing websites for an early childhood classroom. The following should be taken into consideration when determining if the online activities are developmentally appropriate:

- The website should match the instructional goals and theme of the program.
- The learning objectives should match the age group such as picture menus, use of graphics, sound cues, etc. for non-readers.
- The instructions should be auditory as well as simple.
- The website should provide a means for exploration and navigation by the child.
- The activities should be high interest and meet the needs of the child.
- The website should be free of violence and explicit language.
- G. The material on the website should be meaningful to the child and represent what he sees in his real world.
- H. The software should work in a consistent way to avoid causing frustration to the child.

The most important thing to keep in mind when safeguarding children when the internet is being used is to know what each child is doing. Place the computers so that all of the screens can be clearly seen. Another way to safeguard is to bookmark some of the sites that are frequently used. Teach the children to never give out their names, addresses, or telephone numbers when using the internet. Filters can be installed, but these are not necessarily a sure cure for objectionable material. Another step in internet safety precautions is to have the parents sign a permission slip that allows their child to have access to the internet. This permission slip should explain to the parents how and why the internet will be used and what will happen if the internet is used inappropriately.

The following are ways to foster visualization of curriculum content:

- Fill the classroom with many different forms of visual stimuli such as models, posters, magazines, dioramas. The children can even make some of these themselves, which creates further understanding of a concept.
- Make use of videos to show things and places that otherwise would be difficult to reach or find examples of.
- Put up words on the walls that are on sentence strips. Point to the words as things are explained.
- Use visuals to explain concepts. Encourage the children to use their imaginations.
- Teach from different locations in the classroom. Take the class outside for a lesson.
- Provide many different examples to teach a concept, especially abstract concepts.

Dramatic play is important primarily because it is enjoyable. It has also been found to have a positive influence on the physical, cognitive and psychosocial development of children. Play can increase strength and fitness as well as the development of motor skills. It can also increase the development of problem solving, creative thinking, and language. Psychosocial development is fostered by the encouragement of cooperation, sharing, and turn-taking. It has also been closely connected to a higher rate of success in school. Smilansky conducted a study that showed a high correlation between success in school and play. She concluded that adults should put a high value on the play of children.

Sociodramatic play boxes are theme-based boxes of props. Preschool children should be provided with realistic props for their play. Teachers can gather inexpensive materials and set up a specific area in the classroom for dramatic play. Build the props around whatever theme unit is being studied. Provide enough time for play and encourage creativity. Be sure to include literacy and print experiences in every play box. Also include items that will promote character and moral development. By using sociodramatic play boxes children develop assertiveness, which contributes to competence later in life. One concept for play, which was developed by Bredekamp in 1999, is that play should be initiated and directed by child, then supported by the teacher.

There are many different ways to set up centers in an early childhood classroom. The size of the classroom is one of the determining factors. Centers can be either portable or permanently set up. A permanent center should be large enough for three or four children, but it should not overpower the room. They can be situated on the floor or on tables. Decorate the centers with materials that relate to the theme being studied. Tubs to hold materials can be used in portable centers. The tubs can be moved around easily to set up centers. They can be decorated with materials that match the theme, which can then be removed and replaced. Teachers can share these portable centers. The number of centers depends on the number of children in the class as well as how large the classroom is.

Planning, Implementing, and Evaluating Instruction
© Mometrix Media - flashcardsecrets.com/praxisii
Pre-Kindergarten Education

Explain what determines the timing schedule for centers.

Planning, Implementing, and Evaluating Instruction
© Mometrix Media - flashcardsecrets.com/praxisii
Pre-Kindergarten Education

Explain what determines the theme for centers.

Planning, Implementing, and Evaluating Instruction
© Mometrix Media - flashcardsecrets.com/praxisii
Pre-Kindergarten Education

Discuss the benefits of preschool inclusive services for children with and without disabilities.

Planning, Implementing, and Evaluating Instruction
© Mometrix Media - flashcardsecrets.com/praxisii
Pre-Kindergarten Education

Discuss Jerome Bruner's Discovery Learning model.

Planning, Implementing, and Evaluating Instruction
© Mometrix Media - flashcardsecrets.com/praxisii
Pre-Kindergarten Education

List some ideas that can be used to establish a planned learning environment based on the theme of circles.

Planning, Implementing, and Evaluating Instruction
© Mometrix Media - flashcardsecrets.com/praxisii
Pre-Kindergarten Education

Discuss teaching techniques for different learning modalities.

Skills, activities, or interests can be the determining factors for setting up the theme of centers. They can be related to whatever unit is being studied. Examples might be dinosaurs or space. Centers can be related to subjects such as language arts, math, music, etc. A math center might contain clocks for learning to tell time or beads that promote counting. Centers that are skill-based might include activities that would develop tying, zipping or buttoning. One of these centers might also incorporate cooking skills and safety skills or cooperation skills. Finally, centers can be focused on something that the students are interested in. A center that includes toy cars and blocks might stress safety or building skills.

Determining when the children go to centers is up to the teacher. One method is to divide the children up, and the whole class is at one of the centers at the same time. The other method is that while part of the class is at the centers, the other is with the teacher doing small group instruction. One of the most important things for the teacher to do is to set up how long each child will be in a center and how they will move from center to center in an organized way. To begin with, it would probably be better to have a structured method of moving and time allowed at the centers. As the children become more familiar with the schedule, then some method of center assignment charts can be implemented.

Jerome Bruner developed the Discovery Learning model. The main points of this model are as follows:
- It is rooted in cognitive psychology, and children interact with their surroundings.
- The children learn through discovery fostered by manipulation of objects.
- The belief is that children will remember more if they find out things on their own.
- Learning is more successful if there is as least a little prior knowledge. Then the teacher can supply some experiences that are structured and more knowledge is acquired.

Some of the benefits of preschool inclusive services for children with disabilities are as follows:
- Eliminates negative labeling and ways of looking at disabled individuals
- Models that provide examples of adaptation
- Peers without disabilities to interact with and with whom to form friendships
- Provides real life experiences

Some of the benefits for children without disabilities are as follows:
- They have the opportunity to develop realistic pictures of people with disabilities.
- They can develop understanding attitudes about disabled individuals.
- They are exposed to individuals who succeed in spite of their disabilities.

The first technique for teaching to different learning modalities is to provide a structured environment. The learning centers provide experiences for learning in different modalities because of the materials and equipment that are used. Blocks, books, computers, dramatic play areas all provide different learning modalities.

The next technique is to take a look at all the ways to learn that are present. Try to include as many modalities as possible for each concept because children can learn in several different styles. An example might be when the class is learning the letter "A." The teacher can print the letter on the chalkboard or show the letter on a poster (visual). Then the class can repeat the letter orally (auditory). After this, they sing a song about the letter (music). Finally, they write the letter in the air with their finger (kinesthetic).

The last technique is to make use of an exploratory approach to learning that is based on a theme. This theme should be something that the children are interested in and want to learn about. Include as many subjects such as math, social studies, literacy, etc. that are related to the theme.

The following can be used to establish a planned learning environment around the theme of circles:
Art center materials such as wagon-wheel pasta, circular stencils, and many sizes of cylinders
Pouring center materials such as funnels and jars
Circle games, balls, and hula hoops
Home center materials, which might include circular cookie cutters and play dough
Math center materials, which might include circular shapes to count
Science center materials, such as bubble wands of different shapes
Block center materials, including wheeled vehicles, construction paper, and markers to make traffic signs
Manipulative center materials including blocks, beads, and puzzles that teach shapes
Music center that has songs and rhymes about shapes
Fruit that is cut into shapes for snack time
Computer games that allow the child to draw shapes

Discuss strategies that will help preschool children to feel safe in troubled times.

List the skills that preschool children should be working on.

Discuss the skills that should be included in early literacy.

Discuss the current trends in preschool assessment.

Discuss the science processing skills that should be developed in preschool children.

Discuss the skills that should be included in mathematics and science.

Preschool children should be involved in activities that promote learning of the alphabet letters. They should also be working on recognizing the sound of the letters in spoken words. Vocabulary development through the use and understanding of the meaning of new words should be taking place. Basic writing skills should be introduced and practiced. An appreciation of books and language should be promoted by access to and activities involving different forms of literature. The children should also be introduced to activities where math and science skills are practiced.

The following strategies can provide a feeling of security and comfort for young children:

Provide comfort in the way of physical needs, such as hugging and cuddling along with smiles. Provide reassurance to promote the child's feeling of security.

Familiar routines and a feeling of security are the two things that children need most during troubled times.

Do not discourage the child's desire to discuss the things that are disturbing.

Provide a relaxing environment with therapeutic play activities as well as avenues through which the children can act out their fears, such as pretending they are firefighters.

Provide experiences through which the child can see that there are peaceful ways to resolve conflicts.

Guide the child toward maintaining a good perspective about the individuals who may be involved in a conflict.

Observe the children for any symptoms of stress in their behavior.

The current trends in preschool assessment include gathering information from several different developmental areas. There is a movement from the use of just one type of assessment to using assessments that target each child's needs and his environmental background. There is also a move away from norm-referenced assessments. Instead, criterion-referenced assessments are used. Formal and direct methods of assessment once were used, whereas now the trend is toward informal, indirect methods. Testing that is designed to accommodate handicapped children is preferred over standardized testing. The emphasis now is on the strengths of the child, and a team approach is being used to educate preschool children. Finally, the assessment trend is to evaluate the whole child by the integration of cognitive, social, and motor development skills.

Early literacy skills need to be developed in an environment that is language-rich. These skills should include:

Awareness of books and other forms of printed materials
Purpose of printed materials
Ability to recognize letters and simple words
Development of listening comprehension
Extension of vocabulary
Sounds of letters
Print orientation
Beginning sounds of words
Writing one's name

The use of activities that are language-rich help to develop these skills and form the foundation for reading and writing in the future.

The activities included in mathematics and science curriculum for preschool should be based on the interests of the children. Mathematics and science concepts are present in all areas of the classroom and playground. Many activities naturally encourage exploration using scientific investigation methods. Preschool children should have opportunities to develop the following mathematics skills:

Counting together with a knowledge of number meaning
Ability to identify at least two shapes; the ability to make the shapes should also be present
Activities that plant the beginning concepts of adding and subtracting
Activities that develop an awareness of above, below, in front of, and behind
Activities that develop an awareness of length, weight, money and temperature
Activities that promote predicting in patterns

Activities that promote the development of the following science processing skills should be provided for preschool children:

Use the senses to observe differences in objects
Be able to group objects according to certain criteria
Use weight, temperature, length, estimation, and data records
Describe events by drawing and language
Infer and predict what will happen
Be able to define what you do and what you see
After observing, be able to come up with a good idea as to what caused the event
Explore by manipulating and investigating to find answers

Discuss characteristics of auditory, kinesthetic and visual learners.

Discuss the creative curriculum model that is used by many Head Start programs.

Explain the key provisions of Section 504 of the Rehabilitation Act of 1973, and the Education for all Handicapped Children Act of 1975.

Describe a visual learner. Then describe an auditory learner. Finally, describe a kinesthetic learner.

Explain the deciding factors as to whether a child with a disability belongs in a private educational program.

Explain the application of Title III of the Americans with Disabilities Act to childcare centers.

The principles upon which the creative curriculum model is based are as follows:
There are 10 areas: learning–blocks, house corner, toy table, art corner, sand and water table, library corner, music activities, cooking activities, computer corner, and the outdoor corner.
Teachers work with children who are different developmentally.
The environment is adapted to challenge the children.
Parents are included in the learning program.
Teachers have resources such as audiovisual training and manuals.

Auditory learners usually:
- Are comfortable in oral discussions
- Remember by saying things out loud
- Require oral lessons
- Do not find written instructions helpful
- Have conversations with themselves
- Repeat information to learn it

Visual learners usually:
- Remember by seeing visual details
- Require visual lessons
- Don't seem to pay attention because they are doodling
- Have trouble with lectures
- Need to write down information to be able to remember it

Kinesthetic learners usually:
- Choose physical activities
- Prefer to actively take part in the learning process
- Have a need to move around
- Have a tendency to "talk" with their hands
- Need to touch to remember
- Remember by thinking in terms of who did what

A **visual learner** likes to sit at the front of the classroom. This prevents someone or something blocking the face of the teacher. It is important to their learning to be able to read the body language and facial expressions of the teacher. These learners probably learn best from charts and diagrams as well as pictures from text books. Using overhead transparencies is another good strategy.
An **auditory learner**'s best method of learning is by listening to the teacher and the other students. Oral lessons and discussions are both good strategies. Providing these children tapes of lessons and having them read aloud are also helpful.
A **kinesthetic learner** needs to be able to touch and manipulate in order to learn. A hands-on experience is the best strategy for these students. A characteristic of these children is an inability to sit still. They always want to be on the move.

Section 504 of the Rehabilitation Act of 1973:
- It is illegal to discriminate against anyone because he or she has a disability.
- Anyone who has a disability must have an equal chance to receive all programs and services.
- Anyone who has a disability connected to speaking, manual or sensory skills must be provided an aid.

Education for all Handicapped Children Act of 1975:
- Any child has the right to a free and appropriate education.
- An IEP (individualized education program) for each child with disabilities must be on file.
- Parents have the right to see the records, and challenge what is in them as well as changes in placement.
- Children have the right to an education in the least restrictive environment.
- Assessment for these children must be unbiased.

Almost all childcare centers must adhere to the guidelines of Title III. This includes home childcare centers as well. Private schools, restaurants, hotels, and many businesses are also governed by this act. The only exemptions are schools that are run by a religious group like a church or synagogue. If the school is merely housed in a church, it is covered by Title III. The key is whether the school is controlled by the church. Title III regulations have to do with the school's (or business's) interactions with the children, parents, guardians, and/or customers that it comes into contact with.

The first thing that should be considered is an individualized assessment. The assessment should address whether the needs of the child can be met without making too many changes in the school. One method is to visit with others who have given care to the child. In this way, one can make a determination about what the child can or cannot do. Also, information regarding the amount of assistance the child needs can be obtained. One of the most important things is not to make premature judgments about the child and his abilities based on the disability alone. If the child would present a threat to others, then he probably should not be admitted. The same would also apply if the program of the school or the environment would require major changes.

Discuss methods to decide the best learning style or styles for children.

Explain the points of the Education for the Handicapped Act (EHA) also known as P.L. 94-142.

The Education for the Handicapped Act (EHA), also known as P.L. 94-142, includes the following points:

- It guarantees a free and appropriate education for all children ages 5–21.
- The education must be free.
- The students' individual needs are met by services that are appropriate.
- Each child must have an individualized education program in place that states all of the services to which the child is entitled.
- Education must be in the least restrictive environment.
- Parents must be allowed to have an active part in every decision about the child. Their consent is required for every action regarding the child. Parents also have the right to due process.

Observation of a child or children is the best method to determine the best learning style or combination of styles. When observing, it is wise to jot down notes or to have a checklist that can be used to document the child's behavior. Another strategy is to simply classify a group of children first into the major categories—visual, auditory, and motor learning styles. Some of the things to observe should include children's conversations and questions, what types of activities are usually their favorites, most successful form of direction by the teacher, preferred environment (group or independent), and whether they experiment to find answers. Other things to watch are whether the child likes to take part in dramatic activities or building activities. Another thing to observe is how they respond to music.